HAMPTON
CHILDHOOD

PENNY LEGG & JAMES MARSH

The
History
Press

For Tony Hale, part of a new breed in the 1950s: the teenager.

And in loving memory of Edith Ann Marsh (1915-2012)
and Peggy Hale (1937–2013)

First published 2013

The History Press
The Mill, Brimscombe Port
Stroud, Gloucestershire, GL5 2QG
www.thehistorypress.co.uk

British Library Cataloguing in Publication Data.
A catalogue record for this book is available from the British Library.

ISBN 978 0 7524 8285 9

Typesetting and origination by The History Press
Printed in Great Britain

CONTENTS

ACKNOWLEDGEMENTS

Penny and James would like to thank all those who have helped with this project and in particular the following people for their help and enthusiasm, without which the book would have been a lot harder to write. Thank you everyone!

Thanks to Matilda Richards and Lucy Simpkin, our editors at The History Press; *The Southampton Daily Echo*; Julie Green, who always saves the day; Karen Hynes, for access to her wonderful 1950s toy and memorabilia collection; the late Brian Bouden, computer whizz; David St John; Oonagh Palmer at the Milestones Museum, Basingstoke and the Hampshire County Council Museums and Archives Service, who made us very welcome; Charles Elder at the University of Southampton; University of Southampton Students' Union; Tom Lingwood and the Southampton and District Transport Heritage Trust for their swift and cheerful co-operation; Derek Stevens and The Hampshire Constabulary Historical Society; John Allen, for his super liner images; Veronica Tippetts, for saving *Rag Week*; Janita Hendricks and Focus Business Communications Limited; James

Arnold, Licensing Manager at The Royal Horticultural Society, RHS Garden Wisley; Brenda Buchman (*née* Reader), and Debbie and Tony Deacon for the image of the floating bridge and Penny's husband Joe, stalwart as ever and great with a scanner!

Thanks also to the wonderful residents of Southampton, children of the 1950s: Rod Andrews; Edna Bouden (*née* Lane); Janet Bowen (*née* Sturgess); Jim Brown; Diana Baker (*née* Thomas); Tony Caws; Philip Chapman; Paddy Curran; Eileen de Lisle Long; Sue Diaper (*née* Lonnon); David Haisman; Dave Hart; Margaret Hitch (*née* Read); Gill Holloway (*née* Haskell); Michael Holloway; Rosina Le Bas; Paddy Maxwell; Graham Meering; Chris Newman; Glenda Patching; David Preston; Kay Rowe; Myron Sowtus; Brian Stansbridge; Jane Waters and Dave Wooders.

Every effort has been made to track down the owners of images. If we have made any mistakes, please let us know and we will make the necessary amendments.

INTRODUCTION

It is not often that two writers who happen to be friends get the opportunity to work together, so for us this book is something special. James was born in Southampton in 1940, and the 1950s is the decade of his childhood that he remembers most. For Penny, researching and writing about this aspect of her adopted city has been both fun and a revelation.

The 1950s was a decade of optimism for the whole country, not just Southampton. The war was still raw for many, but it had been won. Children in Southampton grew up playing on bombsites until they were cleared, along with the slums, to provide new homes. The school leaving age was fifteen and upon leaving education the majority of children moved into employment. Conscription, brought in as National Service in 1948, meant that any lingering childhood for boys was abruptly cut short at eighteen, regardless of the fact that 'coming of age' was considered as twenty-one.

For many Southampton children, growing up in the 1950s meant short trousers and goosebumps, comic swapping, Saturday morning pictures and, if the family could afford it, the arrival of television. An end to petrol rationing and the appearance of the family car meant that middle-class families could go out more, while most kids were more likely to spend their bus fares on sweets, freely available again after rationing ended in 1953.

Between 1950 and 1964, thirty-two new schools were built in Southampton and the city rebuilt and extended itself, spreading into villages hitherto on the periphery of the city. Southampton's centre was remodelled, and trams gave way to buses in 1948. Tramlines remained well into the fifties, criss-crossing the landscape. Children growing up in this decade were able to witness the start of the transformation of the town from a broken, but not defeated, port to a vibrant maritime hub, which achieved city status in 1964.

We are indebted to a number of local residents who spoke to us about their experiences of growing up in the 1950s in Southampton. Some of what they told us has been incorporated into the text of this book, along with some of the particular memories James has of the decade. We hope that these experiences will help to bring the period alive again for those who lived through the era, and will paint a vivid portrait of the time for those just discovering the magic of the fifties.

Penny Legg and James Marsh
Southampton, 2013

one

AFTER THE WAR

The ruin of the historic Holy Rood Church after the Southampton blitz on 30 November 1940. (Image courtesy of Derek Stevens and the Hampshire Constabulary Historical Society)

Southampton suffered during the Second World War, as did many of Britain's towns and cities. Bombs ruined the historic Holy Rood Church, caused heartbreak by killing children sheltering in the basement of the Civic Centre and left a landscape that would take years to rebuild.

For children, the terrors of the 1940s, when for safety's sake they were often kept very much tied to their mother's apron strings, were replaced by the relative calm of the 1950s – children could be children again.

The war, though, was never far away, as Rod Andrews, born in Sholing in 1946, comments:

> The war was why, when we went into town to the shops, most of Above Bar was single-storey, temporary buildings. For nearly ten years the town centre was one big building site. I loved a trip to town to see the cranes, the cement mixers and the builders.

Above Bar Street, 1955. It took a long time for the city to reach this point – much of this area was destroyed or damaged during the war. (Image courtesy of Julie Brown)

Brian Stansbridge, born in 1951, summed up attitudes in the decade:

> The way that people were supposed to behave (scrubbing the doorstep, sweeping the pavement in front of your house, drawing the curtains on the day of a funeral, clean shoes, giving up your seat to adults on the bus, tipping your cap to school teachers and other adults, holding doors open for people); the things that were taboo (having lilac in the house); things that weren't spoken about (living in sin, extra-marital affairs); feeling sorry for families that weren't quite up to the mark for some reason; disdain for families and kids that were 'dirty' or 'smelly'; severely disapproving of 'wasters' and 'idlers' (people who didn't want to work); shunning families that had had one or more members in prison.

RATIONING

The Second World War had drained this country of much in the way of food, clothing and household goods. Strict rationing of all these commodities was the order of the day and many children had never known any different. Families were registered at one particular shop for their meat and groceries; there was no option to move elsewhere. Children running errands would be given the ration book. This was a huge responsibility as all the family's coupons were inside it. Bread rationing, which was started after the war, stopped in 1948 and clothes came off the ration in 1949. However, petrol, sweets, sugar and meat were all still rationed as Britain moved into the 1950s. Rod Andrews remembers rationing well:

> Sweets featured high in our day/week/month. Rationing was still on then. I think it was lifted when I was about eight. [Sweet rationing stopped in February 1953 and sugar rationing ceased in September

of the same year.] My mum was a great innovator and with very little sugar she was able to conjure up her own selection of sweets. She shaped chocolate, sugar and something else into eggs each Easter, using two large spoons to make the egg shape. She made lovely toffee apples that had all my pals queuing at the back door.

For Michael Holloway, born in Shirley in 1939, the end of sweet rationing spelt joy, as it did for many of Southampton's children:

A friend and I rode our bikes to the Cosy Cabin sweet shop in Paynes Road. Mars bars were our target at 4d (2p) each. We were disappointed to only be allowed to buy four.

Petrol was the first of the rationed items to be discontinued in the fifties, on 26 May 1950, which did not mean all that much to the children but meant more to their parents. Money, though, was short in most houses so nothing was wasted that could be used by other people. One thing kids didn't get their hands on was the brown paper bag many shops used for carrying things like biscuits and other loose goods. Parents saved these. They were useful to help take oily stains out of clothing, when placed between the stain and a hot iron. These same bags were also ideal to keep sentimental items in, such as locks of hair or photographs, in chests of drawers in draughty bedrooms – central heating was only a dream and frosty windows and overcoats as eiderdowns were reality.

Children earned the 3d (1p) deposit back on their father's beer bottle when they returned it to the pub, and they soon found a use for the daily newspaper; each edition was hoarded until there were enough copies to make a run to the fish and chip shop worthwhile. Old rickety prams, soap boxes, wheelbarrows if you could find one, were all eagerly seized upon and piled high with paper. Once at the fish and chip shop the paper could be exchanged for a coveted bag of chips. If you were lucky, a bag of scraps, the crispy bits of batter that broke off the fish during frying, were on offer and were scooped up, bagged and eagerly scoffed by small mouths! Rod Andrews remembers another fish and chip shop treat – nothing was wasted. 'On Saturday mornings we would ask the man who owned the shop if he had any fish left over and for 3d we indulged in a few pieces of cold battered fish … we loved it.'

Mothers often made their own chips, as this was cheaper than the chip shop, easy to do and went a long way to filling their children's empty stomachs. There were no ready meals available then, until the advent of things like beef burgers (the first Wimpy bar opened in 1954 in London), so doing it yourself was the norm. James remembers family meal times:

> My mother was very good at getting a few extra potatoes each week and as there were four children in the family then – my brother, two sisters and me – she did chips at least twice a week. She fried these in a big saucepan and once they were ready she took two eggs and broke both of them into her large frying pan. Then, breaking the yolks, she fried these in one big piece. Once cooked, the eggs were divided into four equal pieces and served to the four of us with the homemade chips. No one could tell us that egg and chips was not a good meal to have because all four of us loved it and never left even one single chip on the plate.

Vegetable peelings and food scraps were saved in a separate container to the household rubbish bin. Everywhere that food was prepared had the bins, which included schools and households. Local farmers or council employees collected them once a week and the scraps were used to feed pigs. James has particularly strong memories of this practice:

The food waste was taken to a council depot in Kent Road, just yards from the houses in Belgrave Road [where James lived with his family]. Here it was cooked up and sent to farms all over Hampshire. But when the wind was in the wrong direction the awful pong from this operation wafted over all the houses, meaning doors and windows were firmly shut.

HAND-ME-DOWNS

During the 1950s, hand-me-down items of clothing were the order of the day. As nothing was wasted, it made sense to pass out-grown children's clothing on to a smaller person. Rod Andrews remembers cast-offs with a smile. 'A lot of clothes I had were handed down from older male cousins. That never bothered me. I was quite proud to wear them.'

However, James's memories are not so happy …

Being a boy growing up in this decade I had to endure this practice all the time. I had an older brother and his clothes were handed down for me to wear. That wasn't so bad, but it was the clothes from other boys in the road that had to be worn as well that caused a feeling of awkwardness that still lingers in the memory today. I can still visualise it now. There would be a knock on our front door and one of the mothers of older boys in the road would be standing on our front step. 'Oh hello, Mrs Marsh,' she would say, 'my David has grown out of these trousers, but there's plenty of wear in them yet. I'm sure they'll fit your little Jimmy a treat.' Then 'little Jimmy' would be sent upstairs to try them on, coming back down, now wearing them, to be subjected to a close scrutiny by my mother and whichever neighbour it was who had brought the trousers for me. 'Oh yes,' they would both chorus, 'they fit him a treat.' So next day off I would go to school wearing trousers that had so recently been the property of one of my or my brothers' friends in our road.

It wasn't just trousers of course that were handed down in this way, but shirts, socks and even shoes travelled around from boy to boy, and the girls were given dresses, blouses, cardigans and footwear in the same manner.

We all had to put up with it, but there is definitely something rather embarrassing about wearing trousers that had belonged to a boy who might be walking alongside you as you walked to school, knowing that as recently as just a few days ago these same trousers had covered his legs. Ah well, that was life!

1940s CHILDREN

Those born in the 1940s noticed a difference between their childhood and those of children born in the following decade. This was because children of the forties had to be sheltered during the dark days of the Second World War. True, it was the continued bombing of Southampton that caused so many buildings to be smashed into ruins (which would later become cherished playgrounds), but during those times when there was a constant threat of bombs being dropped on the town, children were kept under their mother's beady eye, much more so than in times of peace. As a result, in the years following the war children grew up much faster and became more streetwise. In this way, the children born in the fifties had a distinct advantage over their slightly older companions.

PLAYTIME

Throughout the 1950s, much of the children's playtime happened outdoors, in empty roads that were free of parked cars.

Homemade bikes were often ridden up and down, making a fearful noise because they sometimes lacked anything as grand as tyres. However, Southampton at that time had a playground that children took full advantage of – the use of the many bombed and empty buildings, many of which remained into the 1960s. These were limited only by the children's imagination, so were, for example, hideouts for baddies and the town jail when playing cowboys and Indians. Brian Stansbridge, brought up in Stratton Road in Shirley, describes the bombsites as 'adventure playgrounds for boys (and some girls)'.

Where I lived, in Stratton Road, there was a small bombsite on the corner of Lion Street and a much larger one at the bottom of Stratton Road, adjacent to the Scout Hut. There was another in Victor Street, opposite the bottom of Stratton Road. They all contained bricks and large chunks of masonry, timber, rusting sheets of corrugated iron, and household items like mangles and tin baths (few of our houses had bathrooms so we would have a bath in the kitchen with water drawn from the 'copper', the gas-fired boiler) and other remains from the ruined homes. The sites were also very overgrown with waist-high weeds, trees and shrubs and always mauve *buddleja* (there was a story that the *buddleja* came from the German bombs – seeds being used as some kind of packing – but I don't think that was true). We would build dens from the wreckage, hidden in amongst the weeds and the shrubs; we would create rope swings hanging from the branches of the trees; we would build camps – a ring of pieces of masonry like a prehistoric stone circle – light a small fire in the middle and sit around like cowboys or soldiers; we would crawl around on our hands and knees in amongst the waist-high weeds creeping up on each other and ambushing passers-by.

Many of the children in the 1950s remember the *buddleja* growing on the sites of bomb craters. (Image courtesy of The Royal Horticultural Society, RHS Garden Wisley)

For reasons I didn't entirely understand, the people who lived next door to bombsites were always cross when they saw or heard kids playing on them and we were always told to 'clear off'.

Janet Bowen (née Sturgess), born in 1937, also remembers the bombsites. 'I had fun playing on these near Radstock Road. The thing I remember most is the abundance of *buddleja* that grew there.' Paddy Maxwell, born in 1949, and who lived in Rossington Way in Bitterne, remembers:

Where I lived, we had woods and glades that stretched from Midanbury to Lances Hill. We had a stream and a site called 'the dump' (Hum Hole, near Lances Hill) where we found old abandoned war stuff, camouflage, bits of aeroplane and even live ammunition, which had to be neutralized by the Army, but it was mainly all kinds of useful bric-a-brac that meant endless hours of fun as we played our boyhood games.

Air-raid shelters did not disappear overnight. Many Anderson shelters remained in private gardens for years after the war, sometimes being used as garden sheds or children's Wendy houses. Public shelters were similarly in evidence.

Brian Stansbridge had a public shelter in his road, opposite Wellington Street and next to Brown and Harrison's Dairy who were renowned for their delicious 3d bottles of orange juice.

It was set into the ground so that only the top two or three feet showed, with a thick concrete slab on top. Interestingly, we never played in it. It was dark and often had a few inches of water in it and seemed very scary. We would venture down into it if dared by a friend, but always got out rapidly as soon as the dare had

One of the huge air-raid shelters erected in Belgrave Road and used by the residents while sheltering from German bombs. (Image courtesy of the Ford Family Collection)

been carried out and honour satisfied. It was almost as if the walls still echoed the fear that its wartime occupants would have been feeling. Eventually, it was demolished and the site used for an extension to Brown and Harrison's.

The choice of games played on the sites, and in the streets generally, reveals the understanding the children had of what had occurred. Rod Andrews remembers:

We all played at war … dividing into German, British or Japanese troops. Guns were either shop bought with precious pocket money, or handmade – as long as you could point it and make a gun noise yourself, you were lethal. Once TV and comics came into our lives we converted, without a backward glance, to Cowboys and Indians.

James remembers:

> Playing in the many bombed buildings that littered Southampton
> was a temptation no red-blooded boy could resist, although we
> all knew it was not allowed. This time it was the police telling
> us this and not our parents. These ruined buildings became our
> camps where we could believe the building belonged to us, and
> if it still had a banister intact we could all slide down it, a thrill
> most children were forbidden at home. All over Southampton
> kids in large numbers enjoyed this. The peril here, though, was
> that if a police constable did catch us they dished out immediate
> punishment – a clip round the ear with a rolled up leather glove.

Concrete anti-tank blocks, known as 'Dragons' Teeth', were still in
place about the city, and these too became a play area for children,
as they jumped from one to the other. At the end of the blocks
were open bays, like shelters but with no windows, and they were
open all round. These made great places for kids to meet up.

BONFIRES

The bombsites were all over Southampton, offering children
endless excitement. However, there was a more practical side
to having them in the area, as Di Baker, (*née* Thomas), born in
1948, remembers:

> Before November even arrived, all the people in our
> neighbourhood would start collecting their rubbish and piling it on
> the bombsite in the corner of St Edmunds and Clarendon Roads
> in Shirley. For bonfire night, we would make a guy out of clothes
> from the rag bag and wheel it around in the traditional hunt for

'a penny for the guy.' Only the dads were allowed to throw the guy onto the bonfire and to light the fireworks.

Margaret Hitch (*née* Read) was born in 1948 and grew up in Argyle Road in Newtown. She remembers sitting in her pushchair on a trip with her mother to the post office in London Road, with the family ration book. She also remembers the bonfires on the old bombsites, 'With everyone's rubbish building up there in the few weeks before Guy Fawkes' night.'

Paddy Maxwell loved bonfire night and remembers it well:

The planning for bonfire night usually started around about September. We would keep our eye open for anything flammable, old car tyres were a particular prize, linoleum, old carpets, bundles of paper, in fact I realise that many garden sheds were cleaned out and given to us eager workers. There was no worry about pollution then with every chimney belching smoke. It was just another addition to the foggy nights that winter months usually were. Building the bonfire was, in a way, teaching us to work together. Leaders emerged and different gangs of lads competed with each other to see who could bring the most stuff to the 'bommy'. We would always say we would not light the bonfire until 9 p.m. on the big day but the excitement was so great that as soon as it was dark we lit the monument we had been building for months and watched it perish to ashes in a few hours. Most lads went out with a guy asking, 'penny for the guy?' Passers-by would give a few coppers that soon added up and were spent, not usually on fireworks but on sweets from Fancy's open-all-hours shop.

It took many years for the city to get over the sheer scale of the bombing. The people of Southampton, though, carried on as usual, as Tony Caws remembers of the mid-fifties:

Above Bar was just one big bombsite. Woolworths had a small, single-storey store a few yards from Pound Street but from their store down to Hanover Buildings there was nothing. There was, though, a wooden footbridge that allowed customers to cross the bombsite to refresh themselves in The Warrens public house.

The deadly legacy of the war lingered on for many years. Myron Sowtus was born in Southampton in 1952. He and his family lived in rented accommodation in Shakespeare Avenue in the Portswood area of Southampton. There was a large field in this avenue that today is the site of the local Jehovah's Witnesses Hall. While playing in this field as a child, young Myron found, to his huge delight, a live bullet. This may have dropped from an aircraft during the war. Myron tried to do what other boys did when given a chance like this and that was to try to set the bullet off, not realising the danger. The trick was to stand the bullet on its pointed end and strike the blunt end with a hammer or a large rock. 'I was banging the end with a stone. Fortunately, one of my uncles was passing at the time and took it from me.'

War inevitably throws up heroes and stories that catch the public's imagination. James remembers his days as a member of the legendary Dambusters! A film, starring Michael Redgrave and Richard Todd, which brought the exploits of this group of flyers to the masses, came out in 1955.

Boys especially had a love for everything that involved water, except, that is, when we had to wash in it. All of us at one time or another, found rivers and streams we could dam. This was such a lot of fun for us as we would wait for a big build-up of water then break the dam and watch this cascade away, sometimes catching us in it if we weren't fast enough to jump out of the way. But this didn't matter. We were the Dambusters doing what 617 Squadron did in the war.

There was always at least one who would fall in when we did this
and also when swinging on a rope across wide stretches of water.
Boys in their underwear were common sights and when seen
it was also noted that a full set of outer clothing was hanging up
somewhere to dry!

Good behaviour was very important during the 1950s and
was drummed into children's minds. 'Never make a nuisance of
yourselves to grown-ups', 'Keep the noise down', and 'Always
show respect for neighbour's property' were the maxims of the
day. All children in this decade kept strictly to these rules with no
deviations at all, of course … well, not many, but kids will be kids
after all! A little bit of mischief did creep in now and again.

Boys and girls played the rough and tumble games such as
cowboys and Indians, cops and robbers, and pirates. In these a great
deal of chasing took place. The cops chased the robbers, cowboys
fought off the Indians, and pirates boarded the ships they were
attacking and took control of them. Of course, when these chases
took place, something as trivial as looking where you were going
didn't come into consideration. Therefore, when looking out of
their back windows into their gardens, often after spending a long
time digging and planting these, and many still with their air-raid
shelters in situ, neighbours were horrified to see large numbers of
children racing over their freshly dug gardens in hot pursuit of their
quarry. These chases often rang with dire threats about what the
grown-ups would do to the kids if they caught them!

TOWARDS ADULTHOOD

The year 1952 was a momentous year for several reasons
in Southampton. One being the official opening of the new

Southampton Technical College (renamed Southampton City College in 1995). The college had grown from the Junior Technical School that had come into being in 1943 and had catered for up to fifty thirteen to fifteen-year-old boys. The school hoped to try to fill the technical skills shortage that the war had revealed and offered two-year full-time courses. It went on to offer part-time and evening courses and took over running day-release courses from the University College. By 1945, the school had progressed to become a Secondary Technical School. It offered 'mathematics, science and drawing office practice, instruction in erection work, metalwork, plumbing, carpentry and joinery.' (*Memories of Southampton*, 2002) In addition, courses on Saturdays were run for adult craftsmen, and building and engineering courses were also held for apprentices. In 1949, the technical school, which up until this point had been housed in premises on Albert Road and Latimer Street, expanded into the old St Mary's workhouse, which was given a radical overhaul. When the school opened in its new premises it had been promoted again and was now the Southampton Technical College. By 27 June 1952, the day of the official opening of the St Mary's premises, the college was offering a wide range of courses to both sexes, from baking and confectionary to Sanitary Engineering, and Southampton's children, young adults and adult population were able to take full advantage.

From 1948 those conscripted to Military Service became National Service personnel. Conscription in the UK ended in 1960, with the last conscripts ending their service in 1963. The school leaving age was fifteen so many youngsters went straight to work immediately after they finished school.

Tony Caws was fifteen in 1953.

When I left school I went straight out to work. At first I worked for Dunning's butcher shop, which was on the corner of Lumsden

Avenue and Shirley Road. There I had to work on Saturdays, delivering, on the carrier bike, customers' orders in the morning and early afternoon, then giving the shop and equipment a very thorough scrubbing the rest of the day.

Dave Wooders, whose family had been left completely destitute by the bombing of Southampton, left school at fifteen and worked at the Dolphin Hotel for a few months as a commis waiter, then went away to sea on the *Queen Mary* for three years as a bellboy. As the Merchant Navy was a reserved occupation, he was not called up for National Service.

In Southampton, as elsewhere, many eighteen years olds found themselves in a whole new world, moving through the no-mans-land between childhood and adulthood in one giant bound. In an

The Dolphin Hotel was immortalised by the fact that Jane Austen celebrated her eighteenth birthday dancing in the hotel's ballroom. Note that the spire of Holy Rood Church is still intact. (Image courtesy of Julie Green)

Pictured here in 1954, Dave Hart was called up at the age of eighteen. He had never been further than Winchester, 13 miles away. He found himself in Kuala Lumpur!

age when cars were still for the better off, most youngsters had often not been further afield than Winchester, thirteen miles away. Local lad Dave Hart was working in Maypole's, the grocer's, when he was called up on 15 July 1954.

I didn't feel too bad being called up. We used to go to the Guildhall dances every week when we were that age. Everyone in Southampton used to queue to get in there Saturday and Wednesday evening and everyone was going off to the Hampshire's to do their bit.

For Dave, National Service held a big surprise as he found himself as the stores man in the clothing store in Wardieburn Camp in Kuala Lumpur, where he was stationed for eighteen months. This was a far cry from his less exotic Southampton life. 'We all buckled down and did it. I was frightened more than anything else because I got shouted at a lot.'

Fellow Southampton-born lad Jim Brown, now a celebrated local author, was also called up for National Service in the 1950s. Having matriculated from Taunton Grammar School, he entered the Army on 20 July 1950. He found himself posted to the Royal Army Education Corps (RAEC) after basic training with the 60th Rifles in Winchester. 'We had three months intensive training in how to kill in various ways: bayonet, Bren gun, Sten gun, hand grenade and, of course, rifle!' It was a far cry from school life in Southampton!

Jim found himself teaching in Paderborn, Germany after intensive classroom training and proudly wore sergeant's stripes as a regimental schoolteacher. At eighteen, it was his job to get soldiers through their Army Certificate of Education. Southampton and childhood must have seemed a long way away.

Jim Brown in 1950, aged eighteen, whilst on National Service. A local German photographer took this shot in exchange for a tin of Nescafe coffee.

Tony Caws served a plumbing apprenticeship, which delayed his call up for National Service. He served three months in the Army, after which he was demobbed because of a medical problem.

I was called up for National Service in September 1959. I suppose that I didn't really mind doing my bit. We were all in it together. There was not much that you could do about it so you just got on with it. There was a little annoyance though. I had just worked for five years for not very high wages and just when a good wage was looming I was called up. The wage in the Army at the time was twenty shillings and sixpence a week. They then stopped one shilling for 'Barrack Room Damages' though, as far as I know, neither I, nor any of my fellow servers, actually damaged anything. The Army also stopped one shilling

The *Queen Mary* at sea. Her three funnels made her instantly recognisable on the Southampton Docks skyline. (Image courtesy of John Allen)

and sixpence per week to cover the cost of a haircut! I was enlisted in the Royal Army Service Corps, nicknamed 'The Galloping Grocers' as they supplied the transport for all the necessary bits and bobs. We were stationed at Blenheim Barracks in Aldershot.

It was not just the conscript that was affected by being called up for National Service. Eileen de Lisle Long remembers her family's reaction to her brother's call up. 'When I was eleven my brother Alfie was called for National Service, and my mother and I were in tears when I inadvertently laid the table for four people instead of three.'

There was no doubt about it; the Second World War had a profound effect on the city that lasted for many years. It left its mark on the landscape and the residents. Children, though, with a growing number not having experienced the horrors the conflict brought, knew no different. They accepted what was and made the best of it.

two

KIDS WILL BE KIDS

Most of the people who experienced childhood in the 1950s remember the decade warmly. After the perils of the forties, the fifties was an era of increasing wonder. As the decade advanced, so did technology and it was this that brought change – and a smile – to many Southampton's children's faces.

NEW TOYS

The fifties was the decade when innovation hit the toyshops. In an age of austerity following the Second World War, advances in scientific knowledge (often made as a result of some wartime breakthrough) brought fun to the nation's children – and the children of Southampton were determined to join in! Plastics were improved and the imagination of toy inventors grew.

Bakelite, the early plastic from the 1930s, was made into Bayko, a system for building houses using moulded bricks and lethal-looking steel pins. It was extremely popular with 1950s children, as Rod Andrews remembers:

Bayko, the popular children's building toy. One wonders if the children playing it were disappointed with the size of the results when compared to the size of the picture on the box! (Image taken at Milestones Museum, courtesy of Hampshire County Council Museums and Archives Service)

My cousins passed on to me their spare Meccano and Bayko and I revelled in building things. Bayko was quite fascinating with those steel bars and slide-in bricks. I spent hours on rainy days making some ramshackle edifices with a combination of Bayko and Meccano.

David Preston, born in Swathling in 1946, remembers Meccano well:

You could build anything. Bridges, cranes, and you learned how to use tools. My brother and I had a chest that my dad made and it was full of Meccano, electric motors and batteries. Dad played Meccano with me. 'I'll help you son,' he would say.

Meccano – Dad's would often offer to 'help' their children with the intricacies of building with this popular system. (Image taken at Milestones Museum, courtesy of Hampshire County Council Museums and Archives Service)

Michael Holloway remembers Meccano and Bayko well:

> My friend David Stubbs, who lived in the downstairs flat, would
> buy the Meccano magazine each month. The latest Dinky Toys or
> Supertoys were always advertised inside the front cover. A cousin
> owned a Bayko building set and when visiting her we used to play
> with it. It consisted of Bakelite pieces, which fitted between steel
> rods that were held upright in holes in a base piece. There were
> brick pieces, windows, doors and a roof. I doubt if the toy would
> be allowed today as the steel rods might injure young children –
> funny how that never happened to us.

Dinky Toys arrived on the scene in the 1950s and were instant
hits. For Rod Andrews, these miniature cars were a big delight:

> Dinky Toys were important. I relied on family cast-offs mainly, but
> pocket money would be saved to buy a new acquisition. Racing cars
> were the number one in the want list. I can still see a racing car that
> was coloured British Racing Green – that was the best and fastest
> in my collection. We wandered around the streets flicking the cars
> with our thumbs, having races that seemed to last for hours.

Dinky modelled cars that were replicas of real life cars; this was
what gave them their appeal in an age when to own a motorcar
was still something that marked the owner out as wealthy. They
were made with great attention to detail and they gave children
the opportunity to study them at close quarters. Many kids
had enviable Dinky collections and proudly kept them in their
bedrooms at home, many keeping the boxes they came in as well.
Sadly, once they had raced down the gutters they often ended up
looking like battered stock cars!

A Vosper Thorneycroft Mighty Atlar low loader. (Image taken at Milestones Museum, courtesy of Hampshire County Council Museums and Archives Service)

Dinky's commercial vehicles were also popular, and their 1959 Thorneycroft Mighty Antar Low-loader was of particular interest to the children of Southampton. Thorneycroft had been an established business in Woolston on the River Itchen since 1904, when it took over the Mordey, Carney & Co. shipyard, which had been on the site since 1870. Thorneycroft built military and civilian ships until 1966, when it merged with Vosper & Company. In 1970, it became Vosper Thorneycroft and now trades as VT Group. Sadly, the company moved out of Woolston in 2004.

OLD TOYS

More traditional pursuits were still popular, though. Chris Newman, born in 1952 and now a respected musician, historian and writer, has memories of sitting on his father's knee and having stories written by Enid Blyton read to him:

> I had a collection of Noddy books. Dad would read about him to me. I wrote my first story based on the Noddy story where Noddy and Big Ears have their hats blown off. I was seven years old. My teacher would read to us at the end of the day. I fell in love with Enid Blyton – the *Wishing Chair* and the *Faraway Tree* trilogy. I am not ashamed to admit I could re-read them now and still enjoy them. Enid Blyton was my idol in those days.

Enid Blyton first wrote about the little wooden toy Noddy in 1949, in *Noddy's Adventures in Toyland*, and continued his adventures until 1963. Noddy was carved by a toy maker but ran away from him and was eventually found wandering in a wood by a Brownie called Big Ears, who took him to Toyland to live. Here he became a taxi driver. The character was particularly popular in the 1950s.

Blyton also created other popular characters. The Famous Five, who had boarding-school holiday adventures, were always at the very top of the favourite lists. The Secret Seven, a group of kids who got into day school term-time scrapes, featured in fifteen novels written between 1949 and 1963. Each was eagerly read and kids fell in love with the author who was giving them so much pleasure as they read her stories.

The two little pig puppets that loved music, Pinky and Perky, first appeared on the BBC in 1957 and were still playing to children in the early 1970s. They were tremendously popular and their books, toys and records were bought for eager, music-loving children. However, these were not the only puppets to be loved; Muffin the Mule had been entertaining young audiences since 1946 and

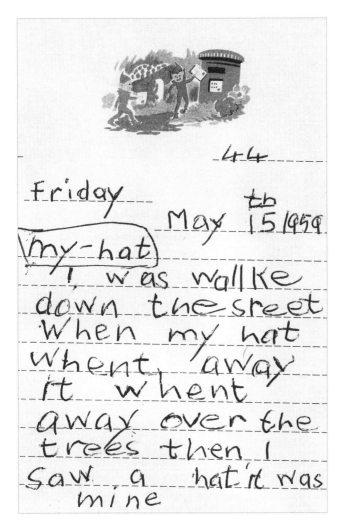

44

Friday

May 15 1959

(my-hat)

I, was wallke
down the sreet
When my hat
whent away
It whent
away over the
trees then I
saw a hat'il was
mine

Chris Newman's first effort at writing a story aged seven, inspired by an Enid Blyton Noddy story. Chris is now a respected musician, writer and historian.

Pinky and Perky with friends. (Courtesy of Karen Hynes)

his programme ran until 1955, when presenter Annette Mills died. Punch and Judy puppet maker Fred Tichner created Muffin, who danced on the piano played by Mills. Puppeteer husband and wife team, Jan Bussell and Ann Hogarth, operated him.

Bob Pelham's (1919–1980) Pelham Puppets' most famous creation was Pinocchio for Disney in 1953, but he made a variety of wooden, brightly coloured puppets from 1947 onwards. They were sold in bright, eye-catching boxes, designed to entice the eager child!

On rainy days children would have to amuse themselves indoors, so they tended to gather in each other's houses and play some of the more popular board games. High on this list were perennial favourites Snakes and Ladders and Ludo. There was a degree of skill in these games – Ludo especially, when it was important to try and knock your opponent's counters off the

A Pelham foal puppet. (Image taken at Milestones Museum, courtesy of Hampshire County Council Museums and Archives Service)

The eye-catching yellow Pelham Puppets box. (Image taken at Milestones Museum, courtesy of Hampshire County Council Museums and Archives Service)

board. Snakes and Ladders relied on getting the right numbers from the dice as it was thrown. Landing on a ladder was good because it moved you up the board and nearer the end of the game, but land on a snake and back down you went.

There were a few, however, who favoured drawing and painting. Most kids at one time or another were given paint boxes as gifts for birthdays or Christmas. These were usually watercolour paints and the boxes they came in also supplied the brush. Hours of fun could be had painting pictures they had created themselves or others from painting books that had the pictures in them, waiting to be coloured in.

As the 1950s progressed, children still made many of their own toys and with it their own fun. Soapbox carts were made from planks of wood and a soapbox at the back to act as the driver's seat. James remembers them well:

> The boys I played with used orange boxes instead of soapboxes and they were just as effective. Boys imagined themselves as the famous racing drivers of the day, winning a Grand Prix against stiff opposition from other drivers, as they raced down a slope in their carts. We had our share of crashes as well, which meant sessions with our mothers to try and explain why our clothes were now ripped and dirty!

Many memories from Southampton's 1950s children are in connection with one of the most important points of growing up in that era – the all-important ability to play in roads that had no parked cars and hardly any traffic passing through them. Glenda Patching, born in 1951 in Bernard Street in the city centre, remembers her peddle car as a toddler. The roads she sedately travelled were gravel, as were many in the area at the time.

Philip Chapman, born in Millbrook in 1949, Brian Stansbridge, Graham Meering (from Sholing) and several other children of the fifties all look back on childhood games in the street with nostalgia. Graham remembers:

> I played tennis in the road with my friend. On summer evenings, all the children would play rounders using a road island as our base. After breakfast I would go out on my bike and not return home until I was hungry!

Kids made their own fun with homemade bikes, footballs, which were usually a jumper or shirt rolled up and filled with newspaper, and cricket stumps comprising three sticks pushed into the ground with a smaller stick on top for the bails. Chasing games were very popular as kids eagerly ran riot, chasing each other around the streets. Girls skipped skilfully; sometimes three at a time, keeping time to rhymes while the rope whirled round and round. Street games that are most often remembered are marbles, conkers, dibs, hopscotch, hoola-hoops and cigarette cards. Hopscotch was recognised as a girls' game but it was one some boys played as well. Myron Sowtus remembers playing street games as a child.

> The skipping rope, something I could never master, was the preserve of the girls and they would have intricate manoeuvres involving three skipping the same rope at the same time, whilst singing songs to the rhythm of the rope. Hopscotch was a game using a stone and numbers chalked onto the pavement's flags. Statues involved a group of children. One would have their back turned to the group and as the group attempted to creep up onto that person they would suddenly turn around and anyone seen to be moving left the game.

Sue Diaper (*née* Lonnon) enjoyed skipping at school. She remembers a skipping rhyme that went something like this, although she did not know at that time what pease pudding was:

> Salt, mustard, vinegar, pepper,
> French almond rock.
> Bread and butter for our supper,
> That's all mother's got.
> Eggs and bacon, salted herring,
> Pease pudding in a pot,
> picked onions, apple pudding,
> We will eat the lot.
> Mabel, Mabel, lay the table
> Don't forget the
> Salt, mustard, vinegar, pepper.

Dibs, enjoyed by both boys and girls, was a game played with five small squares held in the hand, which were then thrown up into the air. The hand was quickly turned over and as many of the dibs as possible were caught on the back. It was a game of skill to try to catch the required number of dibs at a time. Yo-yos were popular and some children were very skilled and could make their yo-yo do almost anything.

Marbles were all the rage in the playgrounds and streets of Southampton. Brian Stansbridge remembers playing them on manhole covers, while Rod Andrews has fond memories of playing in the gutter near his home:

> Marbles (we always called them allys [ah-lees]) we collected and played a lot. They were, after all, cheap to buy and swap. For some reason, we used the street gutters to play the game. One would

flick off their allys and the other would try to hit them. If you hit your opponents' ally it was yours. We used to play all around the side streets, up and down the gutters. Our mums would make a drawstring bag to keep our playing collection in. Again, on rainy days endless hours of fun were had when you lined them all up and counted them and then played games with them in your imagination.

James remembers playing marbles, too:

Each time you hit one you kept it and my favourite was when there were a lot of marbles in the gutter. Then you started to come into your own, hitting one marble with force and sending it crashing into a lot more. The marbles gained with this manoeuvre were plentiful, but of course only if you were successful. If the other boy was good at marbles as well then the losses could be dreadful.

Rod Andrews, meanwhile, remembers other exciting places to play:

Another street 'game' not often mentioned was simply playing in puddles. There were more unmade roads around then and after rain there was always a great choice of puddles. They became our high seas. Boats were made out of anything buoyant – lollipop sticks, tin lids, even kindling was shaped into boat shapes. Sails were made out of old cigarette packets or bird feathers. Stones were moved around to form harbours and channels and, apart from the odd car wanting to get by, we would play uninterrupted for ages. There was a brickyard in the valley near us and it served as our playground. It had undergrowth and trees and a stream, and at weekends we could roam it. We spent most of the summer there, building camps, cooking potatoes in the fire and some of the older ones slept there in the camps we made.

CONKERS

Every year autumn arrived and with it one of the biggest challenges of the whole year – conkers. First they had to be gathered from the trees, and once they were harvested they were hardened either by baking them or soaking them in vinegar – the harder the conker, the more chance of success. If a conker could win at least twenty conker contests it usually meant its owner became the king of the school playground.

Dave Wooders, born in 1941 and brought up in Oaktree Road, Bitterne Park, remembers conkers. He had a tried and tested method for having the best conker in the neighbourhood!

> We used to get a skewer and put the hole in first before it went into the vinegar! A lot of people put it in the vinegar without the hole and then the vinegar couldn't get into it, could it? If you think about it, it's common sense. I might have been devious enough to do that and then bake it in the oven! If you had a twenty-er, you were king! When playing, if you missed and it went round, it would lock together. Cries of 'Tangs!' would go up when conker strings were tangled together.

CIGARETTE CARDS

Cigarette cards were small rectangular pieces of card printed with all manner of pictures and information. They were free inside a packet of cigarettes and were designed to be collected in sets. They were, of course, a means to encourage the purchase of cigarettes. Children's sweet cigarettes, available from all sweetshops, also came with children's versions of the cards, often depicting cartoon characters.

Kids being kids, the cigarette cards became another means of amusement, as James remembers:

It was the competition that was important to us all. My favourite here, because I was fairly good at it, was cigarette cards. These we collected from our fathers because they came with certain brands of cigarettes that were on sale at this time. If your dad didn't smoke the right brand then it was necessary to bargain with other boys whose fathers did. So swapping came into play. Once a boy had a good enough collection it was challenge time, to gain more and end up as the supreme champion with the biggest collection of these cards in your road. The idea was that a few of these cards would be propped up against a wall, some of your own and some of your opponent's. Then, from a set distance away, you and the child you were playing against took a card and, placing it between your thumb and forefinger, flicked it at the cards to try and knock them down. The ones you did manage to knock down you kept. So, if you were a good flicker, you won more cards.

Children's cigarette cards showing cartoon characters. (Image courtesy of Karen Hynes)

MISCHIEF

A favourite bit of mischief for the children of Southampton was the game of knock the door and run away. This meant simply that one child would be selected to knock on a door then swiftly run away to join the rest of his chums in hiding. All would wait and giggle as they watched the frustration of the grown-ups as they opened their doors to find no one there. An extension of this was the devious plan of using a long piece of rope that stretched right across the road. One end of this was tied to the knocker of a door, the other end, with plenty of slack, was tied to the doorknocker of the house immediately opposite. It was then knock on the first door and scatter. When the door that was knocked was opened not only did the grown-up rage to see that, yet again, there was no one there, he or she failed to see the rope that was now stretched taut, with the effect that the door knocker of the house opposite was now pulled up. When the first door was angrily slammed shut the doorknocker opposite crashed down, so that the householders there had the same frustration of finding no one standing on their doorstep. This particular game only worked in the dark evenings of winter and went on until either the grown-ups realised what was going on and angrily cut the rope, while shouting out threats of what they would do to the 'brats' who were responsible for this if they caught them, or if a car came along the road and broke the rope.

In the 1950s, the Sports Centre and the Ice Rink were among the favourite places for Southampton children to hang out. Di Baker grew up first in Portswood and later in Shirley. She remembers the Sports Centre:

> Throughout the fifties we would make the long walk from Shirley to the Sports Centre carrying large cardboard boxes that we had scrounged from the Co-Op in Shirley High Street. They would not

let us on the bus. Usually it was my mother, a neighbour's child and I who went but sometimes several neighbours would come with their children. We went in our everyday clothes – blouse, cardigan and skirt with T-bar sandals because that was all we had. We certainly owned no trousers. Just occasionally, at the height of summer, we would wear our shorts. We would drag the boxes up any slope that looked promising and try to slide down. We did not have to worry about carrying the boxes home, as they quickly became flat pieces of cardboard. All this was great fun and it was free!

Upon hearing Di's memory, James remembers:

Boys slid down steep slopes on sheets of corrugated tin. There was nothing like it as you waited to be pushed off at the top. The wind rushing past your face as your sheet speeded up and the sheer thrill of the speed you were travelling at was a joy to be remembered and cherished. Sometimes the end of these runs were not so good because stopping was not an option if things did go wrong, and if there was water anywhere near the end of a run many children went swimming with their clothes on because they simply couldn't do anything about it.

DAYS OUT

Children in the 1950s were curious about the world around them and particularly the town or city they were born into. Films were being made about some of the world's great explorers and these filled the imagination. One of these, shown at the Saturday morning picture shows that were so popular, concerned the finding of Doctor Livingstone by Stanley, played by Spencer Tracy in the film *Stanley and Livingstone* (1939). Children thrilled to watch this as Stanley and his native bearers slashed their way through dense jungle and kept going until final triumph and those famous words were uttered, 'Doctor Livingstone, I presume.' This was *Boys Own* stuff and many made up their minds that exploring was something they would like to do themselves. When the film of Scott's expedition to the South Pole in the film *Scott of the Antarctic* (1948), starring John Mills as Scott, came out, interest was at fever pitch. Mills, talking to his wife in the film, expressed the reason he was prepared to take on such a dangerous expedition. 'It's those footsteps in the snow,' he says, looking down at his own in the sand of the beach they are standing on. 'Knowing you have made them and they are the first to be left here, it means you are walking on land that no one has trodden on before you.'

Children watching that film took those words to heart and set out to explore their own world with the aim of leaving those virgin footsteps behind them. The trouble here though was that in a built-up area unexplored land was extremely hard to find. But did that stop Southampton's famous explorers? Not a bit of it. The 1950s saw the exploration of Southampton Common, Woodmill and beyond, as well as anywhere else that had enough foliage that children could turn into steaming jungles with dangerous wildlife all around, not to mention native tribes that meant them no good at all! James remembers it all vividly:

I was as good as Stanley and Captain Scott put together and with my trusty partner went fearlessly into uncharted places, boldly going where no man had gone before. My partner and fellow explorer was my trusty friend Edwin Wheeler and between us we discovered Southampton's more densely foliaged and wild parts. For a long time, we had walked the tow path of the River

Itchen from Woodmill up to Mansbridge but only on one side of the river. The opposite bank was much more overgrown, and looking at this one day Edwin said, 'I wonder what it's like over that side.' My chest swelled and my explorer's instinct took over, 'Let's go and find out,' I said. And so started the fearless exploration of the other side of the river, through undergrowth that had never seen a human foot before. We took no notice of the many footprints already here, because, of course, that would have completely spoiled the illusion of our being the first to walk this bank. However, approaching the end of the trek we came on to private land where the salmon fishing takes place and here we were greeted by the angry shout of a man who roared, 'What are you two kids doing here? This is private property, clear off or I'll call the police.'

'Run!' shouted Edwin and we both took to our heels, unfortunately getting too near the bank of the river so, with yells of fright, we both plunged into the water. It wasn't the most successful of exploration adventures as we both plodded home with water running out of our clothes and tried to work out what on earth we were going to say to our mothers when we got home.

This spirit of adventure is what makes children what they are. It doesn't matter if what they are doing is not real as long as it is in their imagination. Explorations over paths that have been in use for years, climbing the highest tree in the world, on the common or elsewhere, or journeying into space, all of these things were achieved in the minds of children as they played out their fantasies.

Family days out were a treat in the decade after the war. Money was short, petrol had only just been made available off the ration, but most families could still not afford to run a car, so the new availability did not make a lot of difference. Di Baker remembers a typical day out:

> A trip to the Weston Shore was a day out. We went there because it was the nearest beach and Mum could organise to meet her sisters and friends who lived in other parts of Southampton there. It also had a playground and the bus fare was not too much. We would walk up to Shirley and than catch the bus down to the floating bridge. Throughout the fifties we went to the Weston Shore, played on the see-saw, collected pebbles of different types and paddled in the sometimes murky water. As we watched the big ships go by, we would wait for the wash to send up bigger waves and we would wave to the rich on the top decks and the migrants on the lower.

Di Baker with her mother Gladys Thomas and Peter Watson, the little boy the family looked after whilst his parents ran the corner shop on Wilton Road, Shirley. They are pictured here on Weston Shore in 1951.

The Weston Shore was a popular place. Graham Meering remembers learning to swim there, and it had a great vantage point to watch the cruise liners as they entered or left the docks in the city.

FOOTBALL CRAZY

Ask anyone in Southampton about football and the majority will smile and say 'The Saints'. The team has held a special place in the hearts of most city residents for over 100 years. The Saints date back to the players of the St Mary's Church football team.

The church itself dates from the Saxon period, although it has been rebuilt several times, with a 200ft-high spire added in 1913. It was badly damaged in the blitz of 1940 but was rebuilt in 1956. The St Mary's Church Deanery Football Club merged with the football club at the St Mary's Church of England Young Men's Association and this evolved into St Mary's FC and then into Southampton St Mary's FC. The team won the Southern League in the 1896-97 season and further amended the name to that which it has gone by ever since, Southampton Football Club, affectionately known as The Saints.

In the 1950s, an age when it was safe for small boys to be taken to the front in order for them to get a better view, while their fathers were happy to stand back and pick them up later, some of The Saints' football matches were particularly memorable. David Bull and Bob Brunskell, in their book *Match of the Millennium*, a look at 100 of the team's most memorable contests, pick out several outstanding games from the 1950s. Some of these were very high scoring indeed and provided the family audiences at The Dell with many thrills as they drank their mugs of Oxo or sucked a boiled mint.

Paddy Curran, born in 1952 and who later found fame as part of the pop group Peter Pod and the Peas, lived at the bottom end of Shirley, near enough to The Dell to hear what went on.

> You could hear the swelling noise from The Dell as expectant fans hoped the latest onslaught would produce a goal. This would either erupt into a huge explosion of noise if the goal materialised or become a quick fade out if not.

On 29 April 1950, when the team was in the Second Division and while The Saints were still smarting over the departure to Fulham of their manager Bill Dodgin, they played Leicester City. They needed to score five goals in the match to have any hope of promotion at the end of the season. Alas, although they threw everything they had into the game, the coveted prize was not to be. Leicester City scored first after five minutes. The home team replied with three goals by the half-time whistle, two from Ted Bates and one from Charlie Wayman, no doubt wowing the 21,091-strong crowd. Bates was on his way to becoming a much-loved figure in Southampton. Wayman, in his last season with The Saints, had been a record £10,000 signing from Newcastle United in the 1946-47 season and had been scoring regularly for his new club ever since. In the second half, each team were to score twice more, making the final score 5–3 to Southampton. It was a Herculean effort but not enough. There had been too many goals scored against the club. As Bull and Brunskell point out, Southampton FC missed out on promotion to the First Division by just 0.065 of a goal. It would be another fifteen years before they did as well again and a further year before they finally made it to the First Division.

The following season, on 18 November 1950, The Saints once again narrowly escaped defeat. They played Coventry City, second in the Second Division, before 22,438 fans in a match described by the *Daily Echo*'s 'commentator' as a 'Game of thrills the crowd liked.' The enthusiasm for the game spills over into the match's coverage, titled 'Ding Dong Dell Saints Win Well!' The legendary Charlie Wayman had moved on (to Preston North End) and been replaced by Edwin 'Eddy' Brown. He had scored in each of his matches to that point and the game on 18 November was no exception, as he went on his way to score twenty goals in thirty-six league matches in the 1950-51 season. By half time, the score was 2–2 with Southampton goals from Brown and Day. The second half was sizzling as goals hit the mark from Jack Edwards, Day once again and then, in the final few moments of the match, Edwards took the score to 5–4. Despite the best efforts of the Coventry goal scorers, Barrett, Ballard, Brown and Norman Lockhart, they were edged out by Southampton's superior goal scoring. The home crowd were ecstatic.

The new decade had dawned and Southampton FC was giving their fans thrills, excitement and entertainment on a grand scale. The Saints would go on to pioneer the use of floodlights in this country in 1951, in a game between the Southampton Reserves and the Tottenham Hotspur Reserves, which Tottenham won with a single goal. They said farewell to Ted Bates in December 1952 as he left his playing days behind to coach the Southampton Reserves. In 1953 the team was relegated to the Third Division and the light of The Saints dimmed.

Brian Stansbridge says of football in the 1950s:

I suppose my abiding memories of football in the fifties are of the legendary Ted Bates, Saints' manager, and Terry Paine. Terry was the subject of a fair amount of pride for Sotonians, as he clearly had remarkable ball-handling skills and, as later proved, when he played for England, he was a football star of international standard. I don't think we had had a player of that calibre before, except maybe Charlie Wayman in the 1940s and very early 1950s.

Terry Paine, born in Winchester in 1939, joined the club in 1956 and went on to appear in 713 league games for The Saints. During that time, he scored 160 goals for the club. He was part of the England 1966 squad.

In the meantime though, a young lad, born in 1945 in Southampton, was busy practising with his football throughout the 1950s. Just as The Saints regained their Second Division position in 1960, he was hoping his local team would be interested in him. They were. His name was Martin Harcourt Chivers.

The 1950s was the decade when playing outdoors, whether in the street or watching professionals on a Saturday afternoon at The Dell, was the thing most kids did, because they could do so in safety. Children could be children.

three

CHILDREN'S IMAGINATION

THE CINEMA

The cinema was an incredibly popular place for Southampton's children in the 1950s. Programmes changed several times a week – Monday to Wednesday one programme played, featuring two films, while from Thursday to Saturday a different programme was shown, and there was another on Sundays.

Saturday morning shows were packed, with small children streaming through the foyers and more piling in through fire exits or other supposedly out-of-bounds alternative entrances, using the cover of darkness to sneak in for free. Films were rated U for universal and were suitable for all ages of viewer; A for Adult and there had to be an adult with the child to be able to view it and X for purely adult viewing. Most children in the fifties went to the pictures alone and never with their parents, so an A rating caused a problem. To get over this awkward situation, kids would stand outside the cinema and wait for a kindly looking adult to come along who was obviously going in, then politely ask if this person would be good enough to take them in as well. This meant handing over the entrance money; kids got in for 9d. Once inside the auditorium, kids politely thanked these adults, took their tickets and disappeared down to the cheap seats to watch the films.

The city had many picture houses, although not all survived the ravages of the Second World War. Southampton's first purpose-built cinema was the Atherley in Shirley. It was the brainchild of William Dalton Buck (1878–1966), a far-sighted cinema enthusiast, and it opened in 1912. The cinema was tremendously popular, showing films to wounded Belgian and Allied soldiers in the First World War, pioneering the use of sound in the 1920s. In the 1950s it was the first cinema to use Cinemascope and stereophonic sound. The cinema had a 38ft-long screen and twenty-four surround-sound speakers mounted on the walls. The Richard Burton, Jean Simmonds and Victor Mature film *The Robe* (1953) was the first film to be shown using the new equipment. In 1950, Ryde Cinemas Ltd owned the cinema and it had 1,092 seats. It played its programme continuously and seats ranged between 1s and 2s 3d.

The Savoy, affectionately known to local children as 'the cabbage', was opened in 1938 in the High Street, Swaythling. David Preston, born in 1946, remembers the cinema well:

> The Savoy, we called it 'the cabbage', was a fleapit. I remember the doorman's name was John and he was a big tall guy. We used to try to sneak in the back and he was always there. We never got away with it. He was everywhere!

The Savoy closed in March 1959 after the last showing of *Bridge on the River Kwai*, starring Alec Guinness.

The Palladium in Portswood is remembered with great fondness. The mayor, Mr Henry Bowyer, opened this fine old cinema in 1913. It is remembered for its glass canopy, which sheltered the pavement and sweet shop outside. The management were proud to advertise their 'flicker free' films and, during the First World War, it too entertained wounded troops.

James remembers the Palladium:

It had a grim and often grumpy doorman who let it be known he didn't like kids. That was alright with us though because we didn't like him either. The cheap seats we all sat in were right in the front of the auditorium and the ones behind this sloped upwards and were much more expensive to sit in. On one occasion, my friend and I decided to be cheeky and slip from our cheap seats into the expensive ones further up. We hadn't even time to settle into these posh seats when Grumpy loomed over us. 'What are you kids doing in these seats?' he roared. 'You're not supposed to be here, let me see your tickets.' We were caught and we knew it. It would now mean a clip round the ear and being thrown out of the cinema, so, with nothing to lose, we decided on cheek. 'Well sir,' I said. 'We were at the front as we should be, but my friend here dropped a two shilling piece on the floor and it rolled up here. We're just trying to find it sir.' There were two things wrong with that statement – one being that neither of us would have had a two shilling piece to drop and the second was that even if we had done the coin could hardly have rolled uphill into the area of the smart seats. We expected an even harder clip round the ear for this blatant cheek, but were amazed when we received sympathy instead. 'Oh sorry lads,' Grumpy said. 'Here, I'll give you a hand to find it.' And he did just that, shining his torch all around the floor. Unfortunately, we had no success in finding the mythical coin but Grumpy let us stay in the posh seats to make up for the disappointment of losing our pocket money.

On Saturday mornings, the large ABC cinemas opened their doors to children who became known as the ABC Minors. ABC Saturday morning pictures took place in Southampton at cinemas like the Plaza in Northam built in the 1930s (one of the few cinemas to be built with a car park), the Rialto built in 1922 in Shirley Road and Mr Buck's second cinema, the Broadway in Portswood. Each child had a badge showing membership of the ABC Minors and those Saturday-morning sessions were a riot of noise, laughter and missiles. The missiles, often dried peas, flew through the air, fired from catapults, so that the inside of these magnificent cinemas were turned into a battleground. Dave Wooders remembers one occasion that got a little out of hand:

I got barred from the ABC Minors. My sister June was a bit of a tomboy. We were upstairs and we were sat there, and she had on a straw boater that girls wore then. She had it hanging down her back on elastic and this nipper behind got hold of it and went ping! She turned round and warned him, 'Don't do that again.' He had his mates with him and ping! The next thing I know, she was out of her seat, she'd got him round the neck and they were on the stairs and she was knocking him one. People came and we were both dragged out and barred. My protests were of no avail. 'It weren't me!' 'You're barred.' We had to go to Portswood on the bus after that and just hang around because we daren't tell our father we'd been barred. I haven't got a lot to say about him, he wasn't a very nice sort of chap. So rather than get told off by him and get a good hiding, we used to just walk about.

At the start of the film sessions, the Minors Song was sung and the lyrics were always shown on the big screen before the showing:

We are the boys and girls well known as
Minors of the ABC.
And every Saturday all line up
To see the films we like and shout aloud with glee.
We like to laugh and have our sing-song;
Such a happy crowd are weee-eeee.
We're all pals together.
We're Minors of the ABC.

Eileen de Lisle Long remembers going to the ABC Minors at the Broadway Cinema with her cousin Pauline:

Children gathered every Saturday morning at the Broadway Cinema in Portswood Road to attend the ABC Minors club, which cost sixpence for four hours of entertainment. The queue waiting for the doors to open was the full length of the cinema on two sides. There were never any parents accompanying the children. The older children looked after their younger brothers and sisters. We each had a card and badge. We used to sing the ABC Minors Song to the tune of 'Bladen Races'. Our card was marked each week we attended and after the card was completely full and the child was old enough and of good behaviour you became a monitor, which entailed keeping an eye on the younger children. We were very proud to become monitors. We all appreciated the cartoons and our favourite films. My favourite was Flash Gordon and the evil Emperor Ming. There was a good selection of films each week: westerns for the boys, Charlie Chaplin and the numerous cartoons Tom and Jerry and Tweetie Pie. When the baddies came onto the screen everyone booed and stamped their feet, and cheered when the good guys won. At Christmas we had a fancy dress parade on stage and Ted Bates, former footballer and manager of the Saints football team, came and presented the prizes, signed autographs and shook hands with lots of children.

The films shown were old, some even silent, but watching Laurel and Hardy, Charlie Chaplin and favourite cowboys such as Roy Rogers, Tex Ritter, Lash Larue and Hopalong Cassidy was very popular. The weekly serial, where the hero was seemingly killed at the end of each episode by going over a cliff whilst trapped inside a car, or being blown up inside a building or run over by a train, was a big hit. At the start of next week's episode, the excited children were shown how the hero miraculously escaped just before the car plunged or the building exploded.

The ABC Minors were the children who went to the ABC cinemas on Saturday mornings. This Christmas shot, taken in the early 1950s, shows a special fancy dress line up. Excitement was high as Ted Bates, former footballer and manager of The Saints football team, came and presented the prizes. (Image courtesy of Eileen de Lisle Long)

The ABC Minors also featured a popular birthday slot. Eileen de Lisle Long remembers it well:

> The Master of Ceremonies was Uncle Bob and each week the children that had a birthday were invited onto the stage and the spotlight was flashed along the line while all the other children sang "Happy Birthday". How important we all felt!

Dave Wooders remembers how the kids had worked out the best way to play the system. 'If it was your birthday you went up on stage and had ice cream. So you would leave it for about three months and then have another birthday! There were so many children.'

David Preston remembers the Rialto. 'Saturday morning it was up the Rialto for the Minors. There was always a Saturday morning serial. They kept you hanging on until next week! I liked Flash Gordon, Hopalong Cassidy and Roy Rodgers.'

Sadly, the Rialto closed in November 1960, after the final film *Around the World in Eighty Days* was shown. The Broadway followed in October 1963. The Plaza had been the first to shut down in November 1957, but it had a new lease of life as it became the Southern Television studios, which began broadcasting on 30 August 1958.

James loved the cinema and the characters had a big impact on him as a small boy. However, he was often brought down to earth with a start:

> The fifties brought us cowboy films and our heroes were Roy Rodgers, Hopalong Cassidy, Gene Autry and Lash Larue. When coming home from the cinema we all played cowboys and Indians and it was the practice to be in the character of your favourite film cowboy. So the shouts went up before the game: 'Bags I, Roy

Rodgers!' The first boy to shout this became the Singing Cowboy for that game. Other names were bagged as well of course, as were some of the more well known outlaws, like Billy the Kid, the James Brothers and Butch Cassidy and the Sundance Kid. Personally, I was never fast enough to get to play my heroes and always ended up being a crook. Many times I was Billy the Kid. Kids all over Southampton played these games of course and many experienced that perpetual nuisance – interruption by mother. You would be deep into outwitting the sheriff and robbing the bank when your name would be called and, looking round, the figure of your mother standing with a shopping bag in her hands meant she wanted something from the shops and it was you who had to go and get it!

COMIC SWAPPING

Many children had weekly comics such as the *Beano*, *Dandy*, *Eagle* and *Topper*. These cost just a few pence and were therefore affordable in most homes. However, American comics were now available in newsagents (and were also being brought over from the USA by many of the merchant seamen based on the port's cruise liners), with titles such as *Superman*, *Batman*, *Spiderman* and *Wonder Woman*. Children were soon eagerly seeking them. These cost the enormous sum of 6d each though, which exceeded the meagre pocket money most kids had in the 1950s. So it was necessary to save up to buy these exciting comics and others featuring comedy characters such as Mickey Mouse, Donald Duck, Porky Pig and Bugs Bunny. Once these comics had been read they were never thrown away because of the trouble and patience it took to acquire them. The answer was to swap them with other children and in this way always have new ones to read.

The favoured swapping place for this venture was outside the cinemas after ABC Minors. James can still visualise the forecourt of the Broadway Cinema at midday on a Saturday with groups of boys looking through each other's collections of American comics before agreeing on a swap:

> There was never any trouble while this took place. Everyone was just content to unload their own read comics and make sure they went home with the equivalent amount of unread ones tucked under their arms. It was a very satisfying way to make sure you always had enough of this wonderful reading material to use up the batteries in your torch as you snuggled under the bedclothes at night. The torch would light up Superman and Batman as they tackled all of the criminals in the United States and set the world to rights.

David Preston also remembers the American comics:

> I had stacks of American comics. They were better than the English comics. The *Beano* and *Dandy* were flimsy paper whereas the American comics were thick, like magazines, and had characters like the Green Hornet, Superman and Batman.

Gill Holloway remembers girls' comics – they were not all aimed at boys!

> I can recall feeling narked that the boys had their own comic the *Eagle* but luckily, quite soon, girls had the *Girl* and the *School Friend*. From memory, the front page was a continuing story of girls at a private school where one was named Imogen, a new name to me. If the girls were being daring then someone would 'keep cave'.

Gill Holloway loved the comics for girls – the aptly named *Girl* and the *School Friend*. (Image courtesy of Gill Holloway)

RADIO

Radio was the main medium of entertainment at home in the fifties. For children, one of the most remembered programmes was *Dick Barton, Special Agent*, which seems to hold a special place in the hearts of many growing up at the time. It's theme tune, the distinctive, exciting and very fast 'Devil's Galop' by Charles Williams, is still instantly recognisable in the twenty-first century, where it has been appropriated by present-day television stars.

Dick Barton was popular on the BBC *Light Programme* between 1946 and 1951, when up to fifteen million listeners would tune in every evening at 6.45 to hear the latest instalment. Indeed, in some areas of Southampton, where forest or fields were to be found, children would listen out for the bell their mother's rang at 6.30 p.m. Kids, of course, had no way to tell the time and would play until they were called in at mealtimes or at night. A lot of the time, mothers would have no idea where their offspring were, so each took turns in going out at 6.30 p.m. and ringing a loud bell. This alerted their children that Dick Barton was about to come on. Boys and girls rushed out of the wooded areas and dived into their own, or friends', houses to hear the next exciting adventure. This practice became a part of children's growing up and the bell became known simply as the 'Dick Barton Bell'.

The story centred on an ex-Royal Marine Commando, Captain Richard Barton MC, and his two sidekicks Snowy White, played by John Mann, and Jock Anderson, played by Alex McCrindle. Three actors played Dick himself over the years – Noel Johnson, Duncan Carse and Gordon Davies. The stories involved the trio fighting crime, getting out of very tricky situations and generally saving Britain from the clutches of unsavoury characters. The show, written by Edward J. Mason and Geoffrey Webb, was sensationalist in nature – its audience lapping up the excitement this generated. The show's catchphrase became 'With one bound Dick was free!' as he escaped from another perilously close shave at the top of a cliff, in a car, on a railway line … Dave Wooders, born in 1941, loved the show; 'It would always end with a cliff-hanger. Snowy, he was Scottish, was his sidekick. Will they get through? Can they be saved? Tune in tomorrow!'

Michael Holloway points out another important point about Dick Barton. 'Listening to the radio was just as important as watching TV in these days. The serial *Dick Barton* which was on the *Light Programme* at 6.45 p.m. helped me learn to tell the time.'

The radio series eventually ceased at Easter in 1951, when its primetime evening slot was given over to a new show that had been running in the late morning, *The Archers*. It was felt that the show's sensationalism was too much and the more conservative show about life on a farm was put in its place. Millions of young fans never forgave the BBC.

Three films were made by Hammer films of Dick's adventures in the late 1940s, one of which was released in 1950, *Dick Barton at Bay*. Production of the films came to a halt when the on-screen star, Don Stannard (1916–1949), was killed in a car accident.

At a time when the space race was just beginning, *Journey into Space* was another highly exciting show enjoyed by youngsters in the fifties. This show, recently rebroadcast on Radio 4 Extra, was the last radio show to bring in more listeners than viewers on the television. It was written by a BBC producer, Charles Chilton and ran for six seasons and seventy-two episodes on the BBC *Light Programme* from 1953. The format was similar to that of *Dick Barton* in that each episode had Captain Jet Morgan (played by Andrew Faulds) and his crew ending in a cliff-hanger. The music (written by Van Philips) was very dramatic. The show was littered with cries of 'Blimey!', 'Strewth!' and 'Good gracious!' as the intrepid astronauts fought the Martians, or any of a variety of other baddies, to save the world. Chris Newman, born in 1952, remembers the show well:

One of the scariest shows of the lot was on BBC Radio (the *Light Progamme*, I think) and was *Journey into Space*. I clearly remember racing home from playing in the nearby fields, so as not to miss a certain episode. Just to find out how Jet, Mitch, Lemmy and Doc were going to get out of whatever trouble they were in this time. Be it monstrous looking (apparently) 'Time Travellers' (Derek Guyler providing the Alien voice) … who were actually trying to help as it turned out … or giant mind controlling Martians wanting to take over the Earth or whatever. The great thing about this show was your imagination having to go to work.

In 1957, the first dog in space, Laika, was blasted into orbit in Sputnik 2, bringing the imaginary *Journey into Space* world a step closer for 1950s children. The *Guardian* reported on 4 November that, 'The second Russian satellite has demonstrated not only that space travel is practicable but that it has come true.' Southampton's kids joined children all over the country in looking forward to being able to go off into the stars and recreate their heroes' exploits.

Another well-loved show was *Educating Archie*, Peter Brough's ventriloquism act for the radio, with his puppet boy Archie Andrews. This started on 6 June 1950 and ran until 1958. The show won *The Daily Mail*'s National Radio Award three years running. When Archie was kidnapped in 1951, millions followed the story and were mightily relieved when the kidnapper left him at the lost property office at Kings Cross Station.

TELEVISION

Television in the fifties was not broadcast twenty-four hours a day as it is in the twenty-first century. Many households did not have a television set, which were built into large wooden housings designed to fit in with the rest of the furniture in an average living room. The Queen's Coronation in 1953 resulted in more households investing in a set, and extended family and friends gathered to watch the wide coverage provided by the BBC. These early sets were all small screened (9 inches) and showed programmes in black and white. Colour television was a long way in the future (the first colour broadcasting came to the UK with BBC 2 in 1967). For working-class families, buying a set was not possible and they had to wait until the arrival of rented sets. In this way, more families were able to crowd eagerly around these small sets and they watched enthralled as the programmes came on. It was just like going to the pictures, but in your own home.

Television proved popular. Muffin the Mule had been a feature of the children's part of the adult BBC programming, in a section called *For the Children* after the war. The arrival of *Watch with Mother* in 1950 brought a regular entertainment and education slot for very young children and was an instant hit. Andy Pandy, the little puppet boy in blue and white striped pyjamas, who lived in a wicker basket, came to the screens in a series of just twenty-six black and white programmes, which were aired repeatedly. Andy's friend Teddy came later, as did Looby Lou, the rag doll.

The 1950s television is a far cry from the sleek, streamlined versions we know today. (Image taken at Milestones Museum, courtesy of Hampshire County Council Museums and Archives Service)

Watch with Mother featured other fondly remembered programmes, too. *Bill and Ben, The Flower Pot Men* 'flobalobed' onto the screen in 1952. Based on the original three stories by Hilda Brabban for radio's *Listen with Mother* in 1951, they were made from flowerpots, with hobnailed boots and gardening gloves for hands. They spoke completely incomprehensibly and so there was a helpful narrator on hand to interpret. They lived in large flowerpots at the bottom of the garden and only popped their heads out of these when the gardener went in for his lunch. These two had gentle adventures, which usually ended up with one or other of the pair having done something naughty. The audience was always asked, 'Was it Bill or was it Ben?' Their friend Little Weed could be relied on to give the warning when the gardener was coming back, so that Bill and Ben could scramble back into their respective flowerpots and hide.

Rag, Tag and Bobtail arrived in 1953 and delighted children with stories about a hedgehog, mouse and rabbit. *Picture Book* was added in 1955. Inside the book children found *Bizzy Lizzy* and her dress with a wishing flower on the front that allowed her to make four wishes. The *Jolly Jack Tars* went sailing to exotic places for adventure. Children were also encouraged to make things using origami or to play memory games.

The Woodentops also arrived in 1955. This happy family firmly reinforced stereotypes and so a generation of fifties and sixties kids learnt that girls were destined to be chained to the kitchen sink, while boys grew up to do 'men's work'. While father was off working on the farm with his farmhand Sam, Mrs Scrubbit helped Mummy Woodentop look after the house and the children. The episode 'Horseshoe', broadcast in 1958, is available on the archive.org website. This story features Spotty Dog singing as he babysits Baby Woodentop for Mother Woodentop! Chris Newman loved *Watch with Mother*.

As a toddler or during infant school holidays, I was one of millions of kids who 'Watched With Mother' at lunchtimes. Actually, I watched with Nanny, my mum's mum, most of the time. I got very disappointed if this programme was replaced with Tennis (Wimbledon) or Test Cricket.

Older children loved shows such as *Billy Bunter*, which ran from 1952 until 1961. Starring Gerald Campion, it was based on the *Billy Bunter at Greyfriars School* stories by Charles Hamilton, writing under his pen name of Frank Richards. Chris Newman says of the show, 'I loved this show and it, of course, featured a fully grown bloke – one Gerald Campion in the title role, who was absolutely brilliant – lifting the character of Bunter straight off of Frank Richards' pages. It inspired me to seek out the books.'

Children growing up in the 1950s had a seemingly limitless supply of energy and imagination. They embraced their world and made of it what they would, taking everything in their stride and enjoying life, just as kids should. They were lucky enough to be at the vanguard of innovation and change.

four

GROWING UP

Growing up meant new experiences – going to school; becoming that newly invented person – the teenager; getting to know and understand the world and how one fitted into it. Southampton was changing slowly as the decade went by. After so much destruction, there was only one way to go and that was up, and Southampton's children took the changes in their stride.

GOING TO SCHOOL

After the war, thirty-two new schools were built in Southampton. These were, in part, to compensate for those damaged during bombing raids but also to accommodate the post-war baby boom. In the late 1940s, in the UK there were almost 900,000 births. This figure was significantly higher than during the war years when couples were separated, or anxiety about the future led to a more cautious approach to starting a family. Millions of men were demobbed and returned home to try to rebuild pre-war relationships or start new lives. The Government responded to the spike in the birth rate by bringing in child benefit and free school milk; this new generation was the future and had to be cherished.

Returning servicemen were given £100 and a civilian suit. Many ended up at the employment exchange looking for work but large numbers were also offered the opportunity to train for professions, such as engineering and teaching. Gill Holloway was born in 1940.

> From January 1950 I was at Bitterne Park Junior School. In the last two years my form teachers were male who, on leaving the military services following the end of the war, had retrained as teachers. On reflection, the final year teacher must have been excellent because the 1951 transfer to grammar schools was outstanding.

SCHOOL LIFE

Speaking to Southampton's 1950s children about school life was revealing. Although this book is not primarily one of reminiscences, the memories shared show the sheer variety of Southampton school experience, good and bad. Most class sizes make a twenty-first century person blink as it was nothing to have forty or more pupils to one teacher and there were no classroom assistants available then! Sue Diaper went to Ascupart Infant School; 'I can remember my first day at school. Mum took me into the hall, which seemed really big, and I had my jam sandwiches with me.'

Not all children embraced school. Chris Newman was born in 1952 and went to Glenfield School, which was built in 1954:

> I was reticent at first because I was so happy at home. It was not that I was a wimp or anything, because I am into everything. I loved it at home and did not want to be bothered with this getting up

and going to school. Why do I want to go to school? The first thing I
did when I went into the classroom – I could not believe the racket!
– I just told them all to shut up! I don't think anyone heard me.

Brian Stainsbridge went to Shirley School, on the corner of Wilton
and Bellemoor Roads. Each of the three separate sections within
the building had its own head teacher and the children, especially
the junior boys and girls, were segregated. The infants were on
the ground floor, the junior girls were on the middle floor and
the junior boys occupied the top floor. Nissen huts were still in
evidence and first-year boys occupied two on a separate site,
on the opposite side of Bellemoor Road. The infants had two
Nissen huts in their playground. The girls and infants shared the
playground to the south of the building and the junior boys had
the playground on the northern side, by Wilton Road. The school
opened in 1912.

Chris Newman's class photograph, taken at Glenfield Infants School in 1959.
Chris is fourth from the left in the front row. Chris was a wolf cub and used his
elasticised green tabs to keep his socks up. (Image courtesy of Chris Newman)

Brian, who was a pupil at the school between 1956 and 1962, has many fond memories of his school days there. He remembers the 'Kind, kind Mr Wheeler', the Shirley Junior Boys head teacher, who kept a donkey as a 'lawn mower' and the 'inspirational' Rodney Spratley, who taught the higher stream class in the fourth year; ran the school choir; directed the school plays; took parties of children on Easter walking holidays to the Lake District and Snowdonia and, on top of all this, always ensured that his students achieved very high pass rates in the 11-plus examination (known to many as 'The Scholarship'). Brian also remembered 'the poor teacher' who was prosecuted for stealing un-drunk school milk, which he took home at the end of the day.

> My first teacher in the Junior Boys was a Mr Walker who was ex-military and looked very stern, but was again very kind. He sucked Meggezone throat sweets all day and had one of the early Stanley knives whose handle you had to unscrew to take out and deploy the blade. He would then carefully sharpen pencils laid out in military fashion on his desk. The whole process fascinated me.

UNIFORMS

Sue Diaper moved up to Ascupart Junior School in 1956; 'Clothes for school were usually a pretty cotton dress with a cardigan and I always wore short white socks. I always had ribbon in my hair and as I got a bit older I had a ponytail instead of plaits.'

Janet Patricia Joan Bowen (née Sturgess) was born in 1937 and lived at 125 Radstock Road, Woolston. She liked her school uniform but it was a headache for her parents:

> The 11-plus exam was several weeks of IQ tests in junior school, then one day to take the English and Maths (arithmetic) exams. I'm sure my

parents were delighted that I'd passed for Itchen Grammar School, as my eldest brother was in the A Level class and my older brother was in Woolston Secondary School in Portsmouth Road. The down side was that they had to apply for a grant for my school uniform. School uniform was a navy gymslip with a maroon girdle, white blouse and maroon blazer with green binding on sleeves and edges and, of course, the school badge with the motto '*en avant*' on it. I liked that motto – forward! Our school ties had a different colour stripe depending on your house. I was a Viking so had a pale blue stripe on mine. The others were: Argonauts, yellow stripe; Venturers, green, and Crusaders, red or it may have been white, I can't quite remember. The summer uniform was a maroon and white candy striped dress.

St Mary's College in Bitterne was split over two locations, the lower school for children aged five to eleven, known as Charlton at one end of Midanbury Lane and the senior, or Main College, at the top. Uniform was brown with gold piping and the college crest on the left breast of the blazer, short trousers, long brown socks and brown shoes. Two further items completed the outfit: a brown peaked cap with the college crest and gold piping and a brown and gold striped tie. Myron Sowtus was at the school in 1957 and says of the uniform, 'I do not recall any disgruntlement about the wearing of school uniform until I got a little bit older when I was longing to move up to the college proper where I could wear long trousers, which were a darn sight warmer in winter. Woe betide you if you were seen outside school not wearing the cap.'

The school uniform at Shirley Junior Boys during the 1950s was, as it is now, green and white. Boys wore short grey trousers, grey or white shirts, a green and white diagonal striped tie and green blazers with an optional green cap. A blue gabardine mackintosh or a camel-coloured duffle coat completed the ensemble.

The blazer and cap badge was a shield with the white intertwined letters SJB, for Shirley Junior Boys. Caps, of course, had to be tipped to schoolteachers and other adults. Brian Stanbridge remembers being kitted out for school:

> I remember my mother taking me to Weaver to Wearer in Shirley High Street each year to buy my new uniform. It was always bought a little on the large side so that I 'grew into it'. Money was tight and uniforms were expensive, but my mother would not have dreamt of turning me out looking less than immaculate.

Paying for school uniforms in an era when money was tight was sometimes very difficult for parents. Credit was often the only way open to cash-strapped families, and the helpful agents from firms such as Russell and Provident were able to supply a need in the city. The 'Provi' agent called regularly at homes. The company dates back to 1880, when an insurance agent working in Bradford, Joshua Kelley Waddilove, was distressed to note the struggle working-class families had to finance essential items like clothes, shoes and furniture. His system of vouchers, that could be exchanged in participating local shops for clothing, food and coal, was a godsend to many hard-pressed families. The vouchers were repaid with affordable weekly instalments, collected by the door-to-door agent. The popularity of the voucher scheme grew and Joshua's company, the Provident Clothing and Supply Company Limited, was the forerunner of the giant Provident Financial Empire known today. Rod Andrew remembers his family using this system:

> Mum paid into a credit system, something called Russell Cheques and another one, Provident Cheques. Russell Cheques were owned and operated by the father of Ken Russell, the film director.

Provident Cheques were, I believe, nationwide. The premise was you bought a two or five pound cheque, for instance, for a shilling and paid the balance off at a shilling a week for the required number of weeks. I am only guessing that a shilling interest was the only interest charged, but on reflection it was probably more than that. You then had to shop only at the shops that displayed the Russell or Provident signs. My annual issue of school clothes and shoes were purchased that way. When my sister won a place at grammar school the extra clothing needed nearly broke my parents; they really struggled.

Mothers in those days certainly did their bit to keep the expenses down, and one practical thing that ensured this was the darning of socks. Boys wore long ones then, because they all wore short trousers, and so the socks were supposed to cover the lower part of the leg. Boys being boys, the socks soon became holey at the heel, probably caused by friction from the amount of running around the average boy did on a daily basis. The nickname for these holes was a 'potato'. The cry would go up in the playground of 'Hey, you've got a potato in your sock!' or 'You've got a spud in your sock!' Mothers would take the offending garment and fix it over a mushroom-shaped wooden object that stretched the heel of the sock across it. Then they went to work, stitching wool in different directions across the hole until the repair was complete. They did a neat job and saved the expense of having to buy new socks for their sons.

GETTING TO SCHOOL

Nowadays it is not unusual for the street containing a school entrance to be lined with cars, sometimes parked half on the pavement and generally causing a nuisance to many other road users as the occupants pick up or deliver their offspring to or from school. In the 1950s things were much different. Most families did not have a car, so arriving or departing from school in such a vehicle was an impossibility. Some children cycled but the majority walked to school, as did Rod Andrews.

> The school I first attended was Victorian and then we moved to new post-war buildings. I attended St Monica School in Sholing and can't remember my mother ever taking me there. My sister attended, so she naturally was stuck with taking me. It was about a mile and a half each way and I enjoyed the walk far more than I did school. When my sister went to grammar school I carried on walking to school with friends.

SCHOOL MEALS

Twenty-first century school children often take their school canteens for granted. With the likes of celebrity chefs championing good school meals cooked in kitchens on site, it is easy to forget that there was a time when school meals were functional and basic, and kids were lucky to have them.

In Southampton, school meals were cooked in centralised council-run kitchens and then transported about the city to the local schools. The results coming from these kitchens were not always appreciated, as James remembers with a shudder:

> Many kids stayed at school and had cooked dinners for their lunch. Parents gave them the money on a Monday morning to pay for a whole week's meals. This should have been wonderful as children are always hungry and a good cooked meal was a great way to satisfy this. Unfortunately, the meals weren't cooked in the

individual schools around Southampton, but in a central kitchen. The food was then sealed in steel containers and taken by vans to the different schools. The result of this being, that after a long time in these containers the food, when dished out, tasted like nothing on earth. Mashed potato should be terrific with meat and gravy but blimey! when it sat on the plate, many a child only ate it because the teachers in charge of the dining areas threatened them with dire punishment if they didn't. Ask many of them today whether they should have chosen the punishment instead of those awful dinners and most will readily agree that they certainly should have done so. Sausages and soggy mash, stew that tasted like diesel oil, and roast dinners that had limp meat, roast potatoes that had been kept warm for ages and were horrible to eat as a consequence, and overcooked, awful cabbage. Would any kids today accept this?

Sue Diaper remembers the one and only school meal she ever had at school:

I can remember wanting to stay for school dinners because all my friends did, but my mum didn't want me to because she thought I'd get upset. I hated custard and we had it the first day I stayed, but I couldn't eat it. My teacher – Miss Platt – made me stay outside the head teacher's room until I ate it, even though it was cold. My mum came to see how I was getting on and found out what had happened. She came in and told the teacher she was taking me home because I was so upset. My teacher said she shouldn't take me home as that wasn't the way to get me to do as I was told and my mum was furious, told her off and took me home for the rest of the day. I never stayed to school dinners again!

CURRICULUM

The Butler Education Act of 1944, named after the Conservative politician Rab Butler, gave all children free education from the age of five to fifteen years, but did not lay down a curriculum. It did, however, introduce a three-tier education system of Grammar, Secondary and Technical Schools. Pupils took the 11-plus examination and the result of that determined which tier they went into.

Many subjects were taught by rote, the endless repetition of facts to embed them into reluctant brains, and mnemonics were often used as an *aide-mémoire*. For example, Richard of York Gave Battle in Vain was used to remember the colours of the rainbow – red, orange, yellow, green, blue, indigo and violet. Girls and boys often studied different subjects, although all had to learn the basics, the Three R's – Reading, Writing and Arithmetic. Brian Stansbridge remembers the appropriately named Mr Clapp, who took his class for music one day a week at Shirley Junior Boys:

> He was a very gentle man. He would either play the piano and get us all singing songs like 'Nick Nack Paddy Wack' and 'Soldier, Soldier Won't You Marry Me', or he would tune into the BBC for a schools music programme, which we listened to on one of those big square plywood speakers.

The pens used for writing were thin sticks with a nib stuck onto the end. These had to be dipped into ink that was in an inkwell, which were in the right-hand corner of every desk. The trouble here was that once dipped into the ink the nib held too much and when the child brought the pen over to carry on writing the ink dripped off and caused an unsightly blot on the paper. Many children were told off for presenting unsightly work and were caned for it. One child, however, had the job of filling the inkwells every day. This was the ink monitor, a job sought after by most kids.

The Broadcast Relay Service, which became Rediffusion, began life in 1928, relaying radio programmes locally in Clacton in Essex. In 1936, the first high-definition radio transmissions began in the London area, broadcast from Alexandra Palace. In 1941, the company's literature explained the benefits of using the Rediffusion system, which carried broadcast programming via wire to homes, schools and businesses across the UK and overseas. The system was simplicity itself, as described on the Rediffusion website:

> The subscriber has no aerial or receiving set to worry about, no valves or batteries to wear out, no need of electric current to operate the set. A loudspeaker with a volume control and a switch is all that is required. The chosen programmes are available instantly on switching on; there is no waiting for valves to warm up.

Thus, the system was very useful for schools and many were equipped with speakers to enable religious services, in particular, to be broadcast.

Paddy Curran, a pupil at Shirley Junior School, remembers that music was always present at school as 'we sang hymns in the morning'; science, history and geography, on the other hand, were introduced into junior schools during the 1950s, as Brian Standbridge comments:

> I think that must have been a relatively new development for junior schools, especially the science, as the school staff made quite a big thing of it. Once we had mastered the theory of

trigonometry, we were all sent off in twos and threes to measure the height of nearby buildings, such as the spire of St James Church – unaccompanied.

Other subjects, like needlework, were kept strictly for the girls, thereby instilling accepted social stereotypes into the next generation. Gill Holloway remembers how this was seen at Itchen Grammar School:

Fashion Design would sound too grand for the 1950s in a grammar school. We called it sewing and it was not favoured as a career subject. My career advice was 'As you are good at sewing then you could consider being a matron in a boarding school!' I shuddered at the thought, as I hated the idea of doing repairs.

Gill Holloway's school photograph, 1954, highlights the incredible talent the teenagers had for dressmaking. She says, 'The girls in the photo are displaying the outfits they have made at school. However, I clearly recall that I wanted to wear a jacket and a skirt, which I had made but the teacher insisted it was to be this dress.' (Gill is seated sulking, centre front).

SPORTS AND SCHOOL OUTINGS

Sport was an important part of the school curriculum. Some schools had to make the best of the premises they had. Sue Diaper remembers Ascupart Primary School: 'I was in the netball and the rounders teams. We used to have a netball practice on the school roof and used to play other schools. Our rounders pitch was in the park.'

Some schools routinely took their pupils out of the school environs for sports lessons. Tony Caws went to the Deanery School, open between 1930 and 1989, in Chapel Road. The school had a sports field behind a high boundary wall – in reality it was a muddy area with the occasional patch of grass. This being the case, sports lessons were on Friday afternoons at Weston Lane School. This involved a journey by bus from Deanery through Bitterne to Weston Lane. It was quite a long journey as the Itchen Bridge didn't exist then and the Floating Bridge was not suitable for a large double-decker bus. Deanery School's 'sports field' was only used for the odd kick-about and PE (or PT as it was then) lesson.

Football was the perennial favourite sport for boys. Footballs were made of leather with an inner tube that had to be blown up. The ball was laced up so that the rubber of the inner tube stayed inside the ball. When the ball got wet, it was very heavy. Football boots, also leather, were not the streamlined footwear they are in the twenty-first century. Brian Stansfield describes them as 'Great clunking things with big leather studs on the bottom. When they got wet they weighed twice as much and you had a job to run in them.'

Girls, in the meantime, were busy playing netball outside or having 'Movement to Music' sessions to music played over the Rediffusion network that most schools had installed.

Dave Wooders attended Bitterne Park Infant, Junior and Senior Schools. At the time, the schools were situated in Manor Farm Road but only the infants and junior schools remain on this site in the twenty-first century. The senior section, now a Specialist Performing Arts and Applied Learning School, stands in Copsewood Road.

> I remember we had huts from the main school. The girls were playing netball outside. Me being dyslexic, I couldn't concentrate too much. I kept looking out the window. The history teacher said, 'If you keep looking out there you will be out there playing with them!' A couple of minutes later, I looked out and the next thing I knew, I was out and playing netball with those girls. I got the micky taken out of me! I was 13 then.

Some schools were adventurous with their trips out. In Shirley, Brian Stainsbridge remembers marathon trips into Dorset or to the Isle of Wight:

> One trip I remember took in Lulworth Cove, Tilly Whim Caves, and Swanage, all in one day. Another was to the Isle of Wight and Carisbrooke Castle. They felt like a big occasion. We paid in instalments I think – maybe a shilling a week for a couple of months. On the prescribed day we would arrive at school early, our duffle bags packed with swimming trunks and towel, packed lunch and a plastic water bottle filled with squash. The coaches would already be parked and waiting on Bellemoor Road. We'd all take our place on the coach and our mothers would line the pavement to wave us off. They were great days and we were allowed much more freedom than kids would be given today. In Swanage, I remember we were allowed to explore the town in small groups, without any teachers, and would only have been between eight and ten years old.

MEDICAL MATTERS

When researching for this book, the authors were sent a junior school class photograph by the little girl in the photo who looked most in the wars – Di Baker. Intrigued by the eye patch, but shy of asking too many questions for fear of embarrassing her, we eventually heard this scary tale of medical care and school supervision in Southampton at the time.

> I had to wear a patch over my right eye because my left eye was lazy and they [the doctors] thought that by making it work harder it would work better. It did not work. This practice made trying to learn to write neatly a near impossible task. It was also at this time that the needle broke off in my arm whilst having my diphtheria vaccination – so I was sent off to school with right eye covered up and left arm in a sling. I promptly fell off the playground equipment and had to have four stitches in my right leg … so I actually looked like Long John Silver trying to impersonate Nelson!

Diane Baker seems a happy little soul in her school photo in 1955, despite having her one good eye covered, to encourage the weaker eye to do more.

Meanwhile, Sue Diaper was in the wars, too:

> I remember falling down the stone stairs in the junior school, and I must have nearly knocked myself out because the room was spinning, I actually saw stars and I felt very far away. I went to hospital in an ambulance for a check up and the doctor said my thick ponytail had stopped the fall from being far worse than it was. He also said I was suffering from concussion.
>
> I remember, too, having my tonsils out at the Children's Hospital. When Mum and Dad came to see me in the evening after having them out, all the other children were sat up in bed waiting for their visitors and I was lying down and not feeling very well with a temperature. I can remember eating some ice cream but I can also remember a nurse holding my nose and trying to make me eat something like custard, which was horrible. I hated custard.

A smartly dressed Sue Diaper in 1952, when she was three years old. Having her tonsils out was an ordeal.

Gill Holloway remembers overhearing a conversation that reveals attitudes to 'women's matters' in the 1950s:

> Whilst waiting at the gate for the paperboy to bring my comic along with the newspaper I've never forgotten the confidential conversation between Mum and a neighbour. The neighbour was seriously concerned because her daughter had wet feet from being caught in the rain and it was during her period. Those were

the days when during that 'time of the month' you could not wash your hair or have a bath and certainly not go swimming.

DISCIPLINE

By and large, children in the 1950s were used to doing as they were told, but misdemeanours, however slight, were punished. In an age before Human Rights legislation, how was discipline maintained in schools? The answer, in addition to the fairly innocent writing of lines and being kept in detention, was often with corporal punishment. A range of implements was available to inflict pain on and instil obedience in pupils, from the palm of a hand to a ruler, a slipper, a belt or a cane.

The fields of Townhill Park estate, 1956. For Chris Newman, going to school was difficult. He had been brought up in the fields and being in school, where noise was loud and discipline was sometimes harsh, was a bit of a shock. Here, Chris or 'The Balaclava Kid' as he calls himself, is four years of age. He was worried about the cows and kept looking over his shoulder. (Image courtesy of Chris Newman)

For some children, never having come across corporal punishment at home, such as Chris Newman at Beechwood Junior School, this came as a shock:

> I was eight years old and they were beating us black and blue – double rulers across the hands. It hurt, particularly on a cold day. Discipline was a good thing but it went too far. The head teacher was a strict disciplinarian. My heart beat faster when he walked by – he was fearsome.

At Shirley Junior Boys School, one teacher, when in a temper, would throw bits of chalk or even blackboard dusters at pupils without too much provocation. Brian Stansbridge remembers one particular occasion there that has stuck in his mind:

> On one occasion, myself and another lad had been sent off to sort out some costumes in his costume store, whilst he continued to teach the rest of the class. After a while, he sent another child down to fetch us back. The child told us that, 'Mr X is in a strop.' When we went into the room he called us to the blackboard where there was a word written in French. He was very angry about something and asked us what we thought the word meant in English. Neither of us had a clue. We received a slap around the back of the head and were sent back to our seats. The word was '*enfant*' and he must have thought the meaning was obvious as it was so similar to the English word 'infant'.

Myron Sowtus remembers his days at St Mary's College, Bitterne in 1957:

> Discipline was very strict, with the leather strap administered upon both hands a recognised punishment. ('10 past 1, Brother

Paul's Office' is still branded upon my memory) and the aim of the teachers with a blackboard duster would put a top darts player to shame. Ducking a piece of chalk thrown because you had been seen talking in class became a skill. Getting slapped on the back of the head was a common occurrence. You did not dare to get caught fighting or you faced the strap or immediate expulsion. Good manners were drilled into you and it was expected that you would stand up when the teacher entered the class, talking in class was a definite no-no, detentions were handed out like confetti and even Prefects could hand out punishments such as writing out fifty times 'I will not run in school corridors'. Funnily enough, these punishments were accepted by every parent without question and supported.

It was not just boys who felt the weight of a heavy hand. Sue Diaper remembers getting into trouble at Ascupart Junior School:

I can remember being smacked at school and it was the only time ever. The whistle had gone and we were waiting for our class to be called to go in and you weren't allowed to move or speak. My friend Linda pushed me as a joke and I told her to stop it and we were both called inside and given a smack! I was heartbroken because I felt I didn't really deserve it. Smacking was common at school and boys got the cane regularly.

SCHOOL LIFE

Life at school, as in other areas, was what you made of it. Some pupils embraced what was on offer and others did not. Many schools had choirs and some of them, such as the ambitious choir at Shirley Junior Boys, tackled quite advanced musical pieces, such as the 'Halleluiah Chorus' from Handel's *Messiah*, a difficult piece to get right for experienced adults, let alone eight to eleven year olds!

Jane Waters, born in 1955, went to Shirley Avenue School when she was four. Her memory is of her teacher, Miss Norah Beck, who ran the school, playing the piano for the school play. School plays were important events. To be in a play was a big responsibility, no matter how large the part played. For Brian Stansbridge, Shirley Junior Boys' school play went straight to his head!

> The greatest triumph was the production of *Noye's Fludde* from the Chester Mystery Plays. I played Noah's son Japhet, who was supposed to be the origin of European peoples. My teacher, Rodney Spratley, decided that I should have red hair, so, without asking my parent's permission, sent me off on my bike to Woolworth's to buy a ginger dye, then dyed my hair in the staff rest room. When I went home my mother almost had a fit, but didn't complain.

Growing up in the 1950s was far from easy and today's politically correct society would probably find much to fault if sent back in time. For the kids of the era though, life was what it was; warts and all.

five

TEENAGERS –
A NEW BREED

LEAVING SCHOOL

The school leaving age in the 1950s was still set at fifteen, with the added incentive that if your fifteenth birthday occurred before the start of the Christmas holidays you could leave then and not have to wait for the end of the school year. Jobs were easy to come by in those days, so school leavers had no trouble at all in finding work. Pupils from Secondary Modern education went straight from school into work. There was none of today's practices where many young men and women go on to university before even thinking about a permanent career. Universities in the 1950s were for those pupils who had passed the 11-plus examination and who went on to grammar schools. Secondary Modern education was very basic; teaching the three R's, of course, and woodwork for boys, with sewing and cookery for girls. There was no opportunity for sitting A levels and other qualifications that would be needed if a university place was considered. As a result, most pupils simply looked forward to that day when they walked out of the playground for the last time and started out in the world of the workplace.

For those few who had gone to grammar school, worked hard for the requisite grades and had a place to study at university, they joined higher education at an exciting stage in its development. On 29 April 1952, Southampton University College received its Royal Charter and could call itself the University of Southampton for the first time.

The university had originally been founded in 1862, using the bequest to Southampton Corporation from Henry Robinson Hartley, the heir to a family fortune from the wine trade. The Hartley Institution was opened by the Prime Minister, Lord Palmerston, and had premises in the High Street. It offered a library, reading room, lecture hall, museum and classrooms. Daytime and evening classes were considered a success, while concerts and lectures were not and were subsequently dropped. At the beginning of the twentieth century, the institute was prospering and had become the Hartley College. It offered daytime degree courses in Arts and Science and evening classes in engineering and naval architecture. Being granted University College status in 1902 further boosted the establishment.

On the eve of the First World War, Southampton University College was officially opened at new and significantly larger premises in Highfield. However, the college was unable to move in as the war led to the site being used as a military hospital. The college was eventually to move into its new premises in October 1919, when there were 300 students. The college flourished and was able to add to its facilities with the £24,500 given by the family of the late Edward Turner Sims. This donation was used to build the Turner Sims library, which was opened in 1935 by the Duke of York, later

King George VI. By the end of the 1940s the college had faculties of Science and Arts and was an Institution of Education. It was now desperate for more space to expand. In 1951, the seeds for the eventual designation as a university were sown when a petition to the King was prepared, asking for the Royal Charter. One of the first duties the new Queen Elizabeth II performed was to sign the charter making the college the University of Southampton.

Rag Week is still an important part of student charity fund raising. This programme of events was printed for the 1954 season. (Courtesy of University of Southampton Students' Union, and thanks to Veronica Tippets for keeping the programme safe)

New students in the fifties found life a mixture of hard work and play. The highlight of playtime was Rag Week. According to Southampton University's own website, Rag Week began in the nineteenth century as a good-natured show of the rivalry between two University of London colleges, Kings College and University College. Students cross-dressed and held mock-official processions, with raising money for charity as the secondary aim. Rag parades became popular further afield, and charity fundraising became the primary purpose of the often madcap events that were planned during the week. Southampton's parade was banned in 1930 for being too rowdy! The parade did not reappear again until 1947.

In 1954, the Rag Day Procession that was held on Tuesday 2 March was billed in the programme as the 'Event of the Year'. It started at 2 p.m. at the university and then proceeded down Winchester Road in Shirley, Commercial Road to the Civic Centre, where the Mayor of Southampton reviewed the parade, before it wound its way back to the university via Bargate, St Marys, Bevois Valley and Portswood.

In 1959, Rag Week was banned after student stunts were thought to have brought the university name into disrepute. Antics like breaking into Parkhurst Prison; leaving graffiti on the

In Southampton, the Procession and the Rag Ball were the two main rag events. (Courtesy of University of Southampton Students' Union)

Businesses in Southampton supported the charitable aims for the Rag activities by advertising in the programme. Mayes was a large department store situated Below Bar. (Courtesy of University of Southampton Students' Union)

Stonehenge site, proving they had been there; unfurling a banner from the clock tower on the Civic Centre and stealing football boots from The Saints players' lockers all contributed to close down the Rag Week high jinks.

By the 1980s the procession was back, and since then Southampton's Rag Week has raised thousands for charity.

The university has continued to prosper with the opening of the Nuffield Theatre on its campus in 1963, the expansion of its undergraduate programmes, increased student accommodation, greater links with local businesses, the opening of research centres, such as the Southampton Oceanography Centre, and, in 1993, the acquisition of the old Taunton's College buildings as additional campus space. By 2001, the student population, both full and part-time, reached 20,000 and has continued to grow ever since.

TEENAGERS

Although the term 'teenage' has been used to describe activities and items relating to boys and girls aged between thirteen and nineteen since the 1920s, the word 'teenager' was not coined until the 1940s. Children simply went from childhood to adulthood, with nothing in between. If a fifteen-year-old boy was as tall as a man, for example, he was a man. The school leaving age reflected this and so he left school to take on adult responsibilities, such as earning a living. Gradually though, the realisation dawned that there was a gap between the immaturity of childhood and the responsibilities of adulthood. This period, when kids dealt with puberty, grew to understand what responsibility meant and learnt how to interact in an adult world, became known as the 'teenage years', and a child going through them was now known as a teenager. Depending on your point of view, this was either an exciting time of being able to explore and experiment, or a miserable time as a child learnt how to cope with the world, spots and all.

According to *Pathé News*, in the decade after the war the earning power of Britain's teenagers was ten times what it had been before the war. Children leaving school found jobs to be plentiful. They could be trained quickly and were soon earning, on average, £8 to £10 a week. This figure is disputed by most of Southampton's 1950s children the authors spoke to, who put the figure at nearer £3 a week. Either way, these earnings gave them a certain amount of spending power and a new place in the order of the world.

JOBS

Many jobs in the 1950s were drastically different from what they are today. Dustmen, for instance, were strong men who carried their own dustbins. They used the back cut ways of many roads in order to gain entry to the rear gardens of the houses there. Once inside, they took the family's dustbin and transferred all of the contents to their own bins. Once this was done, they hoisted these full bins onto their shoulders and went back out into the road where the dustcart waited. Once there, they tipped the rubbish they were carrying into the spaces provided for it on the back of the dustcart. This was hard and very demanding work, as was the job of the coalman, who heaved hundredweight sacks of coal onto their backs before delivering it to homes. For teenagers, just starting out and still maturing, this kind of very hard labour was not for them and other forms of work were looked for.

James remembers:

I left school at Christmas 1955, and lorded it over many of my friends in Belgrave Road who were born in 1941 and so had to wait for the end of the school year before they too could leave school behind them. (I was born in December 1940.) I had no trouble at all in finding work, so once the New Year started, I walked into one of the laundries in Portswood Road and obtained a job as a van boy for Amey's laundry. I worked at this job for at least half of that year and revelled in the fact I was now earning a weekly wage (about £3 10s) a week. I had two more jobs that year. At the offices of the *Southern Daily Echo*, I was in the dispatch room next to the printing presses and boy, did they make a noise! My job was to stand at the end of a conveyor belt and to lift off bundles of newspapers

The Eastleigh railway works, showing the scope of the extent of the railway in the town in the late 1930s, early '40s. Many local children were taken on as apprentices at the works. (Photographer unknown)

for transportation to the many newsagents in Southampton. When I first went there, they thought I was too small and therefore too weak for the job. Newspapers came off the conveyor belt in large bundles that weighed a lot. I was small and skinny but certainly not weak. So I did my share of hefting those bundles from conveyor belt to the loading bays along with everyone else.

Then I worked as a mill boy at a timber yard in Southampton Docks. It was here that my love of ships was rekindled and my dad, at my pleading, got me a place at a sea training school and I went there in February 1957.

LICK 'EM AND STICK 'EM

National Insurance in the 1950s was paid out of your wages by your employers, who bought insurance stamps and stuck them on a card bearing your name and national insurance number. This was the accepted way of doing things so no one had any complaint. But people moved around frequently from job to job and often disgruntled employees would say to these employers, 'Stick your job, mate. I've had enough of it.' Then, thinking of the stamps that were stuck on their cards every week and realising this employer would no longer be doing this, the following command was added: 'Lick 'em and stick 'em!'

OUT TO WORK

Factories, building sites, shops and offices all offered school leavers the chance to start out on their working lives. The later concept of 'work experience' was something that no one had even heard of. Experience was simply gained whilst actually doing a job in the workplace.

Earning money was a powerful draw for a teenager. Gill Holloway was thrilled to get her first job:

> As soon as the law permitted, which I think was age thirteen, I applied for a Saturday job and worked in Woolworths in Above Bar, Southampton. My regular counter was 'Paint and Polish', which also sold Bumpers; these were men's brown canvas shoes. We shop assistants stood in the centre of the counter, which was an arm's length deep, with the merchandise surrounding us. Occasionally, I was transferred to 'Lighting', which was exhausting in the summer because of the extreme heat from the illumination. Sometimes I helped out on 'Biscuits'. A trip to the basement, to restock with paper bags, was a welcome break.

NO CAPS

The 1950s was still the age of the cap for most working-class men. Teenagers from this era, however, would have none of this outdated form of head attire. After all, they had paid for the latest hair fashion and wanted to show this off, so why hide it under a cap? The cap, too, was a symbol of the working classes and was in fact doffed to bosses by the labouring masses. The 1950s started the era of the rebel. Both boys and girls, now out working and earning their own living, refused to be downgraded in this fashion – they were their own people and were determined to let everyone know this. It was the age of the dapper Teddy Boys, their clothes a result of the Saville-Row inspired, upper-class Edwardian style revival in the late 1940s and early '50s. This was appropriated and made their own by working-class London lads, before the style spread to the suburbs and then nationwide. The *Daily Mail* was possibly the first to use the term 'Teddy' in 1953 as a short form for 'Edwardian'. Teddy Girls, sometimes known as Judies, wore pencil skirts and drape jackets, and later the American fashion of full skirts.

A whole culture grew up around young people, with its own fashion, music, dance and thinking. Anyone over the age of twenty was old and consequently, out of date.

New music was radically different from the sedate sounds that had been the norm before in the UK, although American GIs during the war had brought swing dances, such as the Lindy Hop, with them. Paddy Curran discovered the new music by accident. It was to change his life:

> I was unaware that my father had been a musician with a big band, and that with the advent of Rock 'n' Roll, finance dictated that paying four or five musicians greatly outweighed paying thirty. He had to look for employment elsewhere and became a shop assistant at Tyrell's. He always kept a pair of drum brushes by his armchair though and would tap along whenever music was heard on the radio, and later the television. Radio had been our main medium of entertainment in my early years, listening to children's shows such as *Uncle Mac*. Dad had a record player and a collection of records – some old 78s and some newer 33s – these were mainly classical and we would sit together and listen. Things started to change when we got a lodger – a young girl in her early twenties. Suddenly, there was a new type of music wafting around the house – Rock 'n' Roll! Now I was hearing the real stuff – Bill Hayley, Buddy Holly, Chuck Berry and, of course, Elvis. Along with Rock 'n' Roll there was skiffle with the likes of Lonnie Donnegan with his 'Rock Island Line', 'My Old Man's a Dustman' and 'Does Your Chewing Gum Lose Its Flavour (On The Bedpost Overnight?)'. I couldn't afford records in the early fifties but towards the end you could buy cheap floppy records. These were wafer thin and the quality was not too good

but they made a sound. By the end of the fifties, we had a TV. My interest in music had been stimulated and I would be glued to it, watching *Six-Five Special* (1957) and *Juke Box Jury* (1959).

Southampton hosted its share of musical heroes. Tony Caws remembers the shows at the Gaumont, formerly the Empire, and now the Mayflower:

> The one that I remember the most vividly was Bill Haley and The Comets. That was around 1957, I think in February or March time [23 February, 1957]. I, along with several hundred others, queued for hours to get tickets for the show. It was very cold. I was still serving my apprenticeship at the time and I seem to recall the ticket costing me virtually a whole week's wages. There was, I believe, also a British band on the bill, Vic Lewis' Big Band seems to ring a bell, but I could be wrong.

Rosina Le Bas went to the Gaumont Theatre too, where she saw the legendary Eddie Cochrane on stage. Eileen de Lisle Long also remembers the music of the era.

> Rock 'n' Roll was the next exciting part of the late fifties for me. All around Southampton, halls were used for Rock 'n' Roll sessions. The Royal Pier was another place where all the teenagers gathered for a dance session. I thoroughly enjoyed learning to jive and saving up pocket money to buy records by Bill Hayley and The Comets, and Tommy Steele.

The new music went hand-in-hand with trends in fashion. The Teddy Boys, predating the Mods in the 1960s, had started out enjoying jazz and skiffle. They soon took to Rock 'n' Roll. James fancied himself as a Ted:

I was resplendent in a knee-length jacket of either purple or blue, with velvet lapels, black drainpipe trousers and winkle picker shoes. My hairstyle was a 'Tony Curtis' with a quiff at the front and a DA at the back, kept in place by that wonder of the age, Brylcreme. [The use of which gave rise to the nickname 'Greaser'.]

Most Teds had respectable jobs and used their Edwardian dress as an antidote to the grey lives they often led. They were respectful to women, loved their mothers and had good manners. Teddy Boys, though, had a bit of a reputation, no doubt fuelled by the over exaggeration of a small number of incidents in the media. In London, they had been known at one time by the unpromising name of 'Cosher Boys' because of their leaning towards violence and their propensity for carrying weapons, such as coshes and flick knives. As a result, Teddy Boys were often not welcome in pubs, clubs and dance halls. One incident in Southampton, which happened to Paddy Curran, demonstrates how some Teddy Boys spoiled the reputations of all:

I used to use a cut between the rows of terraced houses and once while walking I was set on by a bunch of Teddy Boys. They held a knife at my throat and threatened to kill me. I think they must have been only about fourteen or fifteen and having a laugh, but they sure scared the hell out of me! It didn't stop me being impressed by the Teddy Boys' motorbikes though. I loved the roar of the engines as they rode by.

Chris Newman, though only a small boy when Teddy Boys arrived on the Southampton scene, remembers how he felt when he saw them.

I can remember waiting for the bus to go to Bitterne. We would go to my granddad's on a Sunday and you could see the Teds just walking around in the drapes and the bootlace tie, with long sideburns. I fell in love with the blow waves and quiffs. We would whisper 'They're Teddy Boys.' There was an aura there. The Teds would gather down Cutbush Lane, now Townhill Park. You could hear their motorbikes and they would take their girlfriends there.

Teddy Boys and Girls frequented the city's coffee bars. Coffee, of course, wasn't the only thing on offer, as Coca Cola had gained in popularity and was now being consumed by many teenagers, straight from the bottle in the American way.

DANCING

For girls, the new music brought frothy fashion, as Gill Holloway remembers; 'I went dancing from 1957. Lots of net petticoats under full skirts were essential for dancing and jiving.'

Dancing was the order of the day and the Royal Pier Pavilion was the place to be. Dance nights especially for teenagers started in 1958 and were hugely popular. Teenagers' club nights cost 2/- a ticket and promised jive and rock music from live bands such as the Three Stars, Wranglers and Blackjacks.

David St John is now a versatile comedy entertainer based near Birmingham in the West Midlands. He works across the country doing stand-up comedy and vocals. Originally from Southampton, he started his career when he appeared at the Royal Pier as a ten-year-old boy in 1958. He remembers:

I suppose my first appearance was that of an end of pier act, a phrase that is used to mock certain entertainers in recent years. But I am proud of that title as it fitted me back in 1958. The Royal Pier near Southampton Docks is one of the most loved buildings in the area and holds many memories for dance fans, who would flock to the old pavilion to dance away the hours to some of the best bands around. Many a romance was ignited as couples took to the floor, which was lit by the light of a thousand mirrors from the revolving ball in the ceiling.

The old Royal Pier hosted some great entertainers throughout the post war years, and its best times were during the late fifties of the new Rock 'n' Roll era.

Teenagers who had outgrown the ABC Minors graduated to the senior evenings at cinemas. James's sister Sue's experiences illustrate how popular cinema going was in the 1950s:

My eldest sister Sue was a bit of a rebel and did things that we kids wouldn't dream of doing. Far too old for childish things like the Minors on Saturday mornings, she started going to the Broadway for their Sunday evening programmes. For this it was necessary to queue for the best chance of getting in. She has since told me that she and her friends would arrive at the Broadway no later than four o'clock in the afternoon to get in for the evening performance at seven o'clock.

GOING COURTING

Courting in the 1950s was still very much influenced by Victoriana. There wasn't the need for a chaperone then but rules applied and were obeyed, mostly by the girls, about how far boys could go when romance was in the air. The cinema was the ideal place for boy/girl relations and the price of the more expensive seats was a definite necessity. It was the back row that was the target for many couples. It made no difference what film was showing on the screen because the courting couples took absolutely no notice of it at all. Some cinemas offered double seats in the back row, which made kissing and cuddling all the easier.

The places to meet were the dance halls around the city with the Royal Pier and the Guildhall at the top of the list. In the days before Rock 'n' Roll, large dance bands performed at these venues. A boy would go over to a girl and politely ask her for a dance. Waltzes were a big favourite because it gave boys the chance to hold their girls up close, a thrill for both. Gangs of teenage boys egged each other on to approach a particular girl if she was attracting more notice than any of the others. 'Go on,' they would say, 'I dare you to go and ask her for a dance.'

Getting over this awkward first step was just the beginning of the often long courting ritual that followed. If this was successful then the back row of the cinema or a walk on Southampton Common, after dark of course, were top of the list. Boys often bragged to their mates about successes with girls at places like the common, but sadly these sessions often took place only in the boy's imagination. Some lads had no trouble at all in attracting the attentions of girls; others, though, were nowhere near as successful.

James remembers just such an occasion!

It wasn't a matter of male attraction that brought the attention of girls, but in most cases the boy's looks and his clothes that did the trick. I had the clothes – Teddy Boy draped jacket, drainpipe trousers, thick crepe soled shoes – and a Tony Curtis haircut, so how could any girl resist me? Sadly, the answer to that was very easy indeed. Girls liked to be with a boy who looked and acted grown-up. That left me out, as the small skinny kid I had been had now grown into a small skinny teenager, who still looked like a small skinny kid. What, then, were my chances with girls?

The answer was, none at all. This bothered me a lot and one event that happened on a day out really did upset me.

I was on an outing from the Eastleigh Railway Works, a guest of my friend Edwin Wheeler. Being an all-male outing, stopping at pubs was not only expected but certainly done. In the evening we stopped at a prearranged pub where dancing was put on for us with local girls in attendance. This was where I could come into my own. I had learned a bit about ballroom dancing and with my good looks and trendy clothes how could I fail? I selected one of the more attractive girls and walked up to her.

'Excuse me,' I said, 'but could I have this dance?' She gave me one long look before replying, 'Oh no, go away. I'm not dancing with you.'

I walked dejectedly back to where Edwin was standing and told him, 'That girl isn't worth bothering about, she's too stuck up to dance with any of us.'

He looked at her then astounded me by saying, 'I don't know, I think I'll ask her.'

'You're wasting your time,' I shouted after him, then watched as he did the same as I had done and asked her to dance. I was then struck dumb as she got up and walked out onto the floor with him and started dancing. How could this be happening I asked myself, I'm much better looking than him and a better dancer so why is that silly girl dancing with him after turning me down? The better-looking bit was something of an exaggeration but I was the more accomplished dancer. The problem, looking back on it now, was that youthful look I still had. The poor girl probably thought one of the men on the outing had brought his son or younger brother and the kid was now asking her to dance.

The fair on Southampton Common was also a good place to meet girls and one ruse was to ask a girl if she would like a go on the ghost train. This was a scary place and a girl would often cling to her male companion for support while going through the dark and noisy ride. Add the helter-skelter, where the girl sat between the boy's legs as they sailed down, and romance often followed.

With the advent of Rock 'n' Roll, the dance halls became the place to be and many Southampton couples started out there, on their way to becoming a couple, and eventually marrying and starting a family.

Janet Bowen's tale of teenage courting may sound a little strange to twenty-first century ears:

> I did spend a bit of time hanging around street corners with a friend hoping to see boys that she liked, but soon got attracted to church through a renewed conversion (I went to Church/Sunday school for many years as a young child). I then went to the Methodist Central Hall (now the Community Church in St Mary's District.) Of course, at that time young men were doing National Service and there were lots of boys there from Marchwood Camp and Netley Hospital. The boys had choices too, from Nurses on training. We had a lovely Youth Leader, Noel New, and we would go on rambles, weekend conventions and have regular youth club and youth meetings in church. Walking home from meetings often meant stopping by at a Coffee Shop. I had lots of friendships, mostly with boys from away. I later met my husband to be, a Welsh soldier, when I was nineteen.

COFFEE BARS

During the 1950s, coffee bars in England came into their own. Teenagers from all walks of life used these as meeting places, often because they were too young to go into pubs. This was an era of a new invention, frothy coffee, and it took off with a bang.

Coffee makers (baristas in the twenty-first century) pulled levers on sophisticated coffee machines and produced a steaming cup that was brimming with a healthy froth. Unlike comedian Tony Hancock, who was to famously rebel against the froth in 1960 (*The Rebel*), teenagers didn't just drink any old coffee; it was frothy coffee they wanted and that's just what they got!

In Southampton, one of these coffee bars stood out way ahead of any of its rivals. It was to be found to the left of the Bargate, on the Above Bar side. It was up a short underpass, then down some steps and it was called the Checkpoint Café.

Dave Wooders, a bellboy on Cunard's *Queen Mary*, which regularly plied between the UK and the USA, remembers; 'I was one of the guys who brought Wrangler Jeans over from America and sold them in the Checkpoint Café for a small profit.'

Many American comics were sold there too, as children longed to get their hands on them. If their elder sea-going brothers didn't go to the USA, then they pestered them to buy the comics for them at the Checkpoint. These would have just been brought over and would have been more up-to-date than those on sale at newsagents in this country.

Seaman from all of the major shipping lines congregated in the Checkpoint and each had their own section of seating. There was no fraternising between the various companies at all. Therefore, American comics and Wrangler Jeans were available for sale at the table occupied by seaman of the Cunard Line.

SOUTHAMPTON ICE RINK

Of all the diversions Southampton held for children growing up in the 1950s, the ice rink is the one most often mentioned. Luckily for Southampton, a commemorative sixtieth anniversary book,

The Club, Southampton Ice Dance & Figure Skating Club, History 1952-1988 (Beagle Publications, 2011) by Eileen de Lisle Long and Brian Cox has been produced. The authors are indebted to this, and to the club secretary Edna Bouden (*née* Lane) for information on the rink.

The city lost its very popular ice rink in an air raid on 17 November 1940. That day, over 1,000 people had spent some time away from their worries while taking a turn on the ice. It was the last time they would be able to skate until 27 March 1952, when the replacement rink opened it doors to an enthusiastic public.

Southampton owed the New Sportsdrome Ice Rink to one man, Charles Knott Senior, a local businessman. It was his vision that saw the refrigeration plant from the Purley Ice Rink and steel from the old Supermarine Spitfire factory come together to make a rink that was Southampton's pride and joy. The Mayor of Southampton, Councillor Minnie Cutler, conducted the reopening ceremony and a twenty-minute skating extravaganza followed.

The first ice show was in December 1952, when *Santa's Toy Shop* played to capacity crowds.

To celebrate the first birthday of the rink, an Anniversary Gala night was staged. Fifty young local skaters, aged between four and fifteen, came together to perform a 'birthday party' on the ice. The culmination was the cutting of a huge cake by Charles Knott Senior. Edna recollects:

> I was twelve years old. My birthday was on the 27 March and the ice rink opened on the 27 March 1952. They had a cake and Charles Knott was asked to come and cut it. When he did so, I jumped out of it! It was my one moment of glory!

In 1952, adult skaters paid 2s 6d (12p) for two hours and children were charged 1s 6d (7p). Skate hire was an additional cost of 1s (5p).

Edna Bouden was a regular at the rink and recalls:

> My life was spent at the ice rink two or three times a week and all weekend. I used to go in the morning and when it came to the end of the first session, I would hide in the lockers and I would still be there when they opened up for the afternoon session. I would push my luck and would still be there when the evening session came on and the ice hockey players were on. Wow! They were lovely! I hadn't paid any more money. I was a teenager at the time. Everyone was getting off the bus. They had their skates over their shoulder and everybody was going skating from all parts of the city. It was just the place you went to; a place that everybody went to – a place of fun. I still have the friendships made there, even after sixty years.

The action is captured on film in the first show to be staged at the new Southampton Ice Rink in December 1952. Edna Bouden (*née* Lane) is the skater nearest the camera in the middle row of performers in *Santa's Toy Shop*. (Image courtesy of Edna Bouden and The Southampton Ice Dance and Figure Skating Club)

The father of the Southampton ice rink, Charles Knott Senior, by John Piper. (Image courtesy of Edna Bouden and The Southampton Ice Dance and Figure Skating Club)

December 1953 saw the production of *Icelahoma*. This 'Wild West Ice Variety' involved over eighty local skaters and ran for five evenings from 28 December. It survives in a short film clip that can be watched on the Focusbiz website. This gives a fascinating insight into the popularity of the ice rink. The barrel jumping, wagons on the ice, cowboys and Indians and the dancing horse are highlights! The vintage film showcases the ice-dancing talent that Southampton possessed at that time.

By 1954, skating was the most popular pastime in Southampton and it was noted that on Saturday mornings, which were reserved for children's sessions, 200-300 children were being turned away each week as the rink was at capacity.

The Southampton ice hockey team, the Vikings, were very popular. The name derived from the second-hand kit the Southampton (Saints) ice hockey team, dating from 1931,

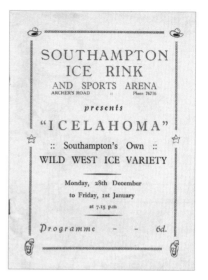

The programme for the ambitious show *Icelahoma*, which featured barrel jumping and a mischievous horse! (Image courtesy of Edna Bouden and The Southampton Ice Dance and Figure Skating Club)

bought from the defunct Club Francais Volants. The kit was emblazoned with the letter 'V', and for economy sake a team name beginning with that letter had to be chosen. The Vikings were born. With the rebuilding of the ice rink in 1952, the club blossomed. It won the Southern Intermediate League and set a record for goal scoring in its first season alone. Throughout the 1950s if you wished to see a Vikings ice hockey game, you had to book a seat in advance.

The ice rink was a popular place for meeting up when Dave Wooders went there as a teenager:

In those days we had a hockey team, the Vikings they were called, so that was their base and the rink was a meeting place. I couldn't skate but it was like an arena so the seats went up and round, a bit like St Mary's football centre. You went up in rows and you could look down. They had a cafeteria. It was a great meeting place for fourteen and fifteen year olds. It was noisy in the ice rink. There were people who could skate, people who would just hang on to the side, and of course, you had all sorts of skaters.

Edna Bouden, thrilled to win the Appleby Trophy for her great passion – skating. (Image courtesy of Edna Bouden and The Southampton Ice Dance and Figure Skating Club)

James remembers the rink, too: 'I couldn't skate. I went with a group of people and they said, "Don't worry, we're all going to go in a line, hang on!" Of course, they went round and I was on the end! It was fast and then I let go.'

The Southampton ice rink hosted a number of competitions and attracted famous names in the skating world. In 1956, Edna Bouden won her first skating award when she won the Appleby Trophy at the rink. She calls the win 'Her most memorable achievement'. She was fifteen.

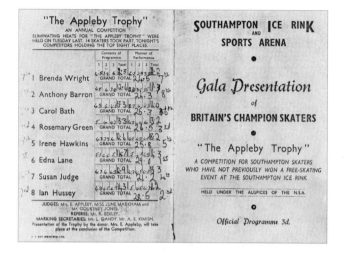

The scoring card that gave Edna Bouden the Appleby Trophy in 1956. (Image courtesy of Edna Bouden and The Southampton Ice Dance and Figure Skating Club)

For Dave Wooders, the Southampton ice rink was to change his life:

> It's strange as it wasn't my idea to go there that night. I was at sea [Dave was a bellboy on the *Queen Mary*] and a chap I used to go to school with said, 'Let's go up the ice rink.'
>
> 'What's it like now?'
>
> 'Plenty of girls!' he said.
>
> Off we went. I had a motorbike, so I had cowboy boots, a black leather jacket with red silk inside, Wrangler jeans, and my black and white check shirt with the pinned down collar. I was seventeen.
>
> So there I was just talking to my mate, Mike Smith and this girl came up. She said, 'You're Dave Wooders. My friend wants to say

The Vikings, Southampton's beloved ice hockey team in 1959. Sadly, the team did not survive the closure of the ice rink. (Image courtesy of Edna Bouden and The Southampton Ice Dance and Figure Skating Club)

hello.' She pointed up the steps and it was quite dark. I walked up and it was Beryl. That is when I first met Beryl, who became my wife.

The ice rink continued to be a popular meeting place for skaters and non-skaters alike until 1988, when the rink was closed without ceremony. The people of Southampton have never forgiven or forgotten the closure and hope that one day a new ice rink will once again grace the city. The Southampton Ice Dance and Figure Skating Club continues to this day, based in Winchester, but the Vikings did not survive the loss of their venue.

SOUTHAMPTON COMMON

Steeped in history, the common was another favourite haunt of children in the 1950s. There is evidence of both Bronze Age and Saxon use of the land, and the Cutthorn Mound, a scheduled Ancient Monument, is the site of the ancient Court Leet. The land was used for animal grazing for centuries, before reservoirs were built to try to supply enough fresh water for the growing town. Following this, the common was planted with trees, and horse races were held there from 1795 until 1889. The common played host to its first fair in 1856. Cricket was first played there in 1874 and football in 1888. The Cemetery Lake was an old gravel pit, flooded in 1881. During both world wars, the area was used to house the military, and between the wars it was a popular sports venue.

The people of Southampton have owned the land since the early thirteenth century, when division of a house and land in the area was in dispute between the Burgesses of Southampton and Nicholas Scherleg, also known as Surlie (Shirley). The dispute was settled in Nicholas's favour but he then granted the burgesses part of the land. It has been loved, and made use of, ever since. Teenagers loved it as a perfect place for an 'after-dark fumble', but it was not just the romantically inclined who were drawn to the open spaces. It was also popular with dog walkers and wildlife enthusiasts too.

In the 1950s, the paddling pool built on the site of one of the reservoirs from the Victorian era was, more often than not,

The popular paddling pool on Southampton Common in the early 1930s.
(Image courtesy of Julie Green)

covered in green slime and was decidedly slippery. Many children who had taken off their shoes and socks to paddle in the pool ended up slipping and getting soaked as a result.

The Cemetery and Bassett Bumps (the result of ancient clay excavations in the area) were a free forerunner of BMX courses and endlessly popular with children and teenagers alike. Brian Stansbridge was a fan: 'It was like a roller coaster ride, but free and you could do it as often as you liked.'

The common's ornamental lake, built as a job-creation scheme in 1888, was the place to try to catch tadpoles, frogs, newts and small fish, such as gudgeon or sticklebacks. In the winter, when the lake froze, brave children ventured out on to the ice but teenagers were more cautious. Brian was one of these would-be heroes.

'We would walk and slide on the frozen lake in winter, which would result in panic when you heard the ice start to crack.'

The funfair was a popular addition to the common on a Bank Holiday. Jane Waters, born in 1955, loved this event:

Dad always took me to the fairs on the common and I used to bring home for Mum the most hideous china Alsatians and various other dogs, which mysteriously disappeared after a time! We would also bring her brandy snaps that were her favourite.

Brian Stansbridge brings the whole occasion to life;

The rides were all great, but the abiding memories for me are the food smells; the people who worked on the rides, who all looked like very dodgy characters, and the stalls at the Cowherd's end [of the Common] that sold cutlery, bedding, tea and dinner sets, toys and clothes. I loved to listen to the banter – just like Dell Boy on *Only Fools and Horses*. The Boxing Booths were fascinating. The boxers would be on the platform outside wearing their shorts and dressing gowns and shadow boxing while the caller drummed up business. He would call for volunteers from the crowd to come and fight one of the professionals. I used to be awestruck when someone went forward, but with hindsight maybe they were plants. I never saw anybody I knew volunteer.

Teenage girls watched mesmerized as their boyfriends fearlessly rode the Jungle Ride – the ultra-fast balancing act with a difference – without holding on. Amazingly, this showing off seemed never to result in casualties!

THE LIDO

Another popular haunt for Southampton's children was the Lido. There had been public baths on the site since 1854, so outdoor swimming was a long-established pastime for the town's residents. The Southampton Public Baths and Wash House Company

An early shot of the popular Lido in the 1930s. (Image courtesy of Julie Green)

originally operated it, but the Southampton Corporation rebuilt it in 1890. Each year, in the third week of May, it opened for the busy summer season, which ran until the middle of September. It closed in 1977.

Rosina Le Bas was born in 1937. Her favourite place in Southampton was the Lido. She spent endless days there with her friends, swimming in the large pools and sunbathing on the terraces. It still holds a particular spot in her memory; 'It was so lovely to be there on a bright sunny day and spend so much time in this marvellous swimming pool. You could meet your friends there as well and the enjoyment we all had was so special.'

Growing up in Southampton in the 1950s meant adapting to huge change, including adjusting to the world of work and of having your own money to spend. This money was a novelty that previous generations would no doubt have envied, as it gave the owner a freedom to develop new ideas that had never been seen before. The results are now in the history books.

six

FAMILY LIFE

Family life was as varied in the 1950s as it is today, with families coming in all shapes and sizes. Myron Sowtus looks back on the decade and sums up the attitudes of the time:

> It is hard to believe that it was not feminine for a lady to be seen smoking in the street, to ever drink from a pint glass or to swear. To have a child out of wedlock was to bring shame upon the family name and as to having been in prison, this was a disgrace. Scandals could be covered up and kept within the family. The father was the head of the household, the mother the home keeper. Manners were everything and women and elders were to be treated with respect.

Many families had to cope with husbands and fathers who were not quite the same as they were when they went off to war. In an age when post-traumatic stress had not been recognised, the effects of what had been termed 'Shell Shock' were difficult to cope with – by both the sufferer and his family. Of the several children who grew up in Southampton during the 1950s and who spoke to

the authors about this aspect of family life, Rod Andrews, born in
1946 in Sholing, spells out some of the problems most eloquently:

> In retrospect I suppose the war loomed large in my early life, though
> I accepted that as normal. The war was the reason there were gaps
> in the houses. The war was the reason there was rationing. The war
> was why Mr X from down the road walked up and down our street
> shouting to himself. The war was why Mrs T stood in the shop with
> tears silently falling down her cheeks. When I asked my mum why
> she was crying, she mouthed, silently, the eternal answer, 'It's the war.'
>
> The war was why my dad hid in the cupboard under the stairs
> and cried when a thunderstorm went over. He would emerge wet
> eyed and visibly shaken as the thunder and lightning had reminded
> him vividly of his time as an artillery gunner in Libya.
>
> My father, like so many other Second World War servicemen
> and women, didn't talk much about his experiences. My father
> would tell us about the silly things he and his fellow captives did,
> but never the gaunt truth.
>
> Normally a quiet, loving and laughing man, I can only ever
> recall him 'losing it' when the Italians were mentioned; something
> sparked off in him whenever pictures of Mussolini came on the
> TV. One day my mother brought two pretty little hand-painted
> plates she had found at the market. My dad turned them over, read
> the words 'Made in Italy' and went out into the yard and smashed
> them. It was only this year, when I am older than my father ever
> was, that I read an account by a fellow gunner who was fighting
> and captured at the same place, same day, in the same desert
> battle as my father [that I understood]. The treatment those men
> received from the Italian troops as they were transported across
> the Libyan desert and then across the Mediterranean to prison
> camps in Italy was disgusting, vile and totally inhuman.

In addition to post-traumatic stress, many families had to cope with major illness. Several 1950s children mentioned that returning fathers were prone to tuberculosis (TB) or other major medical problems. TB, a bacterial infection of the lungs spread by droplet infection, is associated with overcrowding, malnourishment and poor healthcare. It was in 1952 that Ukrainian-American biochemist Selman Abraham Waksman was awarded the Nobel Prize for Medicine for work on streptomycin, an antibiotic treatment for TB. Waksman and Albert Shatz, his student, had developed the antibiotic, although Shatz missed the Nobel Prize as he was classed as a research assistant. Shatz had actually first made the discovery of streptomycin in 1943.

HOUSING

Insufficient housing in the 1950s was a problem after enemy bombing during the war destroyed many homes. In the short term, this was overcome by hastily erecting prefabricated houses, or prefabs as they were known, and, in some cases, by families living in Nissen Huts in Houndwell Park. These huts had been used to house American troops during the war. David Haisman remembers them very well, as he mentions in his autobiography *Raised on the Titanic* (Boolarong Press, 2002). David is the son of *Titanic* survivor Edith Haisman. He went with her to South Africa for most of the war. On returning to England he stayed in a prefab with one of his brothers and his family, before moving to the Nissen hut in the park. In his book he says:

> On leaving the ship that morning, we were met by my brother Leo, his wife and two children and taken to their home, which was known as a prefab. These prefabricated homes were meant

for a family of five. There were now eleven of us cramped into that small home. Eventually, something turned up and we were to finally move out. Our new home was to be a Nissen hut situated in parkland in the middle of Southampton.

The prefabs were built off-site and erected on-site in minimal time. David Preston loved living in his family's prefab.

We were given a prefab and it was wonderful as these had things we never had before, such as fitted kitchens with a gas fridge and a cooker. They also had an indoor bathroom with indoor toilet facilities as well. Gone now were the days of outdoor toilets and a tin bath in the kitchen. In some ways Adolph Hitler did us a favour because bombing our old houses gave us the chance to move into these prefabs and start a whole new way of life.

Tin baths were used in most working-class houses then and water for these was drawn from the gas-heated boiler. The bath was placed in the kitchen and the person using it was then given the privacy to do so. In large families, however, this process would take too long and the water would be cold long before the older children took their turn at having a bath. So it was done two at a time, two girls sharing, one sitting at either end, and then two boys doing the same. As well as saving hot water, it also saved on time, which made sense to do so.

The copper came into its own for the family washing, so on washday (Mondays, whatever the weather) these were heated up and all of the washing, clothes, towels handkerchiefs etc. were boiled clean. Then the rinsing was done in the kitchen sink before the long process of hanging it all out on the line. These stretched the length of the back garden and the clotheslines were raised and lowered by pullies. Everything was pegged onto the line and nature was then left to get on with the job of drying it. On rainy Mondays however, the average house looked like a small laundry as washing was draped around the small fire in the living room to dry – a long and very boring process, especially for children to put up with.

Myron Sowtus was born in Southampton in 1952. His father was Polish, whose immediate family had perished in Auschwitz and Belsen. His mother was Irish. They lived in rented accommodation in Shakespeare Avenue in the Portswood area of Southampton. Myron's mother came from a large Irish family who came to England and all lived in Shakespeare Avenue. It was his grandparents who then ruled the roost, his granddad's word being law. However, his grandmother did most of the cooking and Myron remembers, 'She made her own home-baked bread and the smell when this was baking was heavenly. Her stews were something to die for.'

The Sowtus family moved to a prefab in Lordswood in 1957. Myron remembers the house:

> This had two bedrooms, a kitchen and bathroom with indoor toilet. But only one coal fire in the living room for heating. In winter this wasn't enough, so a paraffin heater was brought in and placed in the hall. All of the doors inside were left open so that the heat from the heater could get into all of the rooms. There was also a large garden and my father, who was a keen gardener, grew lots of vegetables for the whole family to enjoy. We also kept rabbits at the bottom of the garden but they always seemed to be able to escape. It wasn't until much later that I realised they only escaped to the stew pot.

Chris Newman lived in Wakefield Road as a small boy and had the run of the Townhill Park estate nearby. In the 1950s, this was all

Chris Newman's family was large but close-knit. Chris is the babe in his mother's arms in this family shot taken in Chris's Aunty Ethel's living room in Spring Road in 1952. (Image courtesy of Chris Newman)

fields and farmland and was a joy for a small boy to grow up around. He lived in a house with his parents and grandparents, plus an uncle who ate all of his meals with them but slept with another of his relatives further down the road. He was brought up with canaries, budgerigars, cats and a dog all sharing the bursting home.

Sue Diaper, born in 1949, lived with her parents and grandparents in a rented flat in Britannia Road, Northam:

My nan worked in the Gas Works as a carpenter during the war and she had a flat because of this. The flats are still there – right opposite the stadium, home of Southampton Football Club. I lived there until I was thirteen and my happiest childhood memories are of living there.

Sue's recollections of life living in the flat, without what many consider to be basic amenities, may make twenty-first century readers wonder!

> I can remember having gaslights and the gas mantles used to go 'pop' when they burnt out. We had no carpet – just lino – and the walls were painted cream at the top and dark green at the bottom. We had a black range and I can remember Mum heating her iron and the kettle on it, as we didn't have electricity then. The toilet was outside the back door, on the balcony, and we used newspaper for toilet paper. We used to keep a tin bath hung up on the balcony and I can remember it used to take ages to fill it up with hot water. I used to hate having my hair washed, because it was very long and thick and took ages to wash and dry. I had to hold my head over the sink or the bath with a towel pressed to my eyes and Mum used to pour jugs of water over it to wash and rinse it. I must have slept in my parent's room up until my grandparents died, and then I remember sleeping in the small room in an armchair bed.

STARTING OUT

Many young couples starting out on their married life together in the '50s, found that getting a place to live was a very difficult thing to do because of the housing shortage. Many couples lived in one room in either the bride or bridegroom's family home. This, of course, made things cramped for the rest of the family living in the house. James remembers:

> We had a very special front room in our home that my mother kept just for important visitors. My five siblings and I were only allowed in this room for two days at Christmas each year. For most of my infant

and very young years the room was the home of our regular lodgers Mr and Mrs Biggs. They were eventually re-housed. Sometimes whole families found themselves with nowhere to live. If my mother knew any of these people, the invitation was immediately given for them to take up residence in our front room until the situation was resolved. Two of my sisters started out on married life living in that room with their new husbands. This was the way things were done then and somehow, despite the overcrowding, it always worked out all right.

ANIMALS

In the 1950s, animals were kept not just as pets but also as working parts of the family. Dogs were guards for the homes they lived in, while cats were kept for the main purpose of keeping down the mice and rats that infested so many properties then. It was, in fact, unusual to enter a house that didn't have an animal in it for one or another of these purposes.

Chris Newman recollects the patter of tiny feet in his house: 'We never had many pets in the house. Only two cats, one dog, a talking budgie called Paul (Mum reared it from an egg), a chirping canary called Canary (I think it was Peter, actually) and Toby, the tortoise.'

There were also the continual food shortages to be considered and here animals again helped enormously. Chickens abounded in many gardens. They produced eggs all year round and a good dinner at Christmas. James remembers:

Some of my friends in Belgrave Road lived in houses that had chicken runs in the garden. They always had fresh eggs to eat in this way. But these runs had to be kept clean and in more than one case that meant several of us being roped in for this backbreaking job. We would be given small knives and taught how to scrape the droppings off the perches – a hard and terribly boring job that always seemed to take ages to get done. Then there was the task of changing the straw bedding in the nesting boxes. We did get 6d each at the end of these sessions but looking back on it now that has to be considered slave labour. We were always delighted of course to see the shiny 6d piece sitting in our hands and made short work of spending it, a race quickly developing to see who could get to the sweet shop first.

We had the fair that came to Southampton three times a year and here it was possible to enjoy the wonders of horse riding. We did see horses all the time, as delivery men still used them to draw their carts bearing milk, bread, vegetables and coal. But the nearest any of us town boys ever got to riding these wonderful animals was when the milkman let us ride up on his milk float. In our imaginations, we would be driving a wagon in a train across the wide-open plains of the great American West, looking out for Indians who we expected to attack the wagon train at any moment. It was great fun and had the added wonder of a real horse plodding along in front of you. But wagon trains didn't stop as many times as the horse drawing the milk float. At the fair, for just a few pence, you could actually ride a real horse and boy, was that simply outstanding! OK, the animal was firmly in the grasp of a grown-up who led the horse for a short walk along a grassed section of the common then turned around and trotted it back again, but those few moments were magic as the horse moved beneath you and the chance for imagination was simply too irresistible to ignore. I was always Roy Rodgers on these occasions. I may not have been fast enough to shout out his name and then play him in our cowboys and Indians games, but for just a short while on the grass of Southampton Common, the horse I was sitting on was Roy's famous palomino, Trigger, and I was the world famous Singing Cowboy. Well, for at least five minutes anyway.

Myron Sowtus had a different experience where horses were concerned:

> I had my first and last ride when my mother put me up on the milkman's horse. As I sat on its back the animal put its head down to eat the grass and that sent me sliding forward. I was not impressed and I vowed I would never ride a horse again.

Myron also remembers other animals that featured in his young life:

> We had rabbits at the bottom of our garden and my father made a small barrow. I would go with him to gather dandelions, which we wheeled back in the barrow. These were used to feed the rabbits. My father also used the horse droppings as fertilizer for the garden.

Fishing was another means of food supply in those days of shortages but most children simply watched as grown-ups stood patiently, waiting for that tug on their line to alert them that a fish had taken the bait and was now firmly caught. The River Itchen had fish in plenty; so many fishermen would occupy the banks, especially at weekends.

Children, though, loved this river for other reasons. Boys and girls flocked to either Woodmill or Mansbridge to indulge in the art of swimming. Swans and ducks moved out of the way as children jumped from the pipe that was fixed to the side of the small stone bridge that crossed the river here.

Boating was also popular, as James remembers:

> The boys of the Belgrave Gang discovered a boatyard in St Deny's Road that hired out rowing boats. This was Dyers Boat yard. So, after sessions with our mothers where we begged to borrow

enough money for the deposit that was needed, we set out to explore our river from a whole new viewpoint. We had been on the water before on homemade rafts and usually all ended up in the water as these broke apart. But the boats from Dyers were the height of luxury and we had many hours of enjoyment in them. Although we took chances and went into places on the river where we weren't supposed to go, great care was taken of the boats because we loved them so much, and we would have lost our deposit money if damage had been done to them. Going home to tell Mum you had lost her money wouldn't have been the easiest thing any of us could have done. While in these boats, though, we had the joy of seeing the marvellous wildlife all around us; the fish that you can see in the water and the swans, ducks and birds in and around the surface are a wonder to see and did indeed teach all of us a lot as we watched them. No class in school or anywhere else could have taught us so much about life than this.

Farm animals were simply a mystery to many town children and this certainly included those from Southampton. They knew milk came from cows because schoolteachers said so, but what did a cow look like? The only time many children saw them was when they were lucky enough to be taken on a school or family trip on a train or coach (charabanc). Children eagerly pointed out of the window at the cows or sheep in a field, but the functions of these animals was not really apparent to them.

Teenage boys and girls just starting out in the world of work took part-time jobs. Mostly as paperboys and girls, or fishmonger's and butcher's boys, delivering customers' orders six days a week. This was when they got used to being on the wrong side of dogs who were simply doing what they had been taught and were protecting their homes from these invaders. Walking up a garden path could result in a snarling dog rushing to intercept, and the only salvation was the grown-up coming swiftly out to pacify the dog and take whatever it was that was being delivered. James remembers:

I had been a butcher's boy for three years before leaving school at Christmas 1955 at the age of fifteen. In my time in this job, I had come across dogs of all sorts and sizes. I prided myself that I could always win them over with kindness by offering my hand to them in friendship and this worked many times. My first full-time job though, in January 1956, was as a van boy for Amey's laundry, going out on a daily basis delivering clean laundry and collecting the soiled things that needed to be taken back to be washed. Dogs, of course, featured largely here but one thing sticks in my mind more than anything else. Our biggest day of the week was Thursday when we went out of town and the round took longer to complete. We always ended up in the village of Hamble. Here I knocked on the door of a small pub with their clean laundry ready for delivery. The pub was not open to the public when we got there so I was let in to the public bar to swap the clean laundry for the soiled to be taken back. The pub had a very large Alsatian dog (known as a German Shepherd now) and it sat just behind the bar as the landlady and I did our business with the laundry. I always knew it was there because from the time I entered the bar until leaving again it never took its eyes off of me.

One week, I was feeling hungry and I looked at the pork pies that were on a dish with a glass lid on the bar. Without a thought, I said to the landlady, 'Can I buy one of these pies please?'

'Yes, of course,' she said, 'help yourself.'

So I reached out and lifted the glass cover and was reaching inside to get one of the pies when the dog leaped up and lunged at me. It was all the landlady could do to get the snarling animal back before managing to sooth it enough for it to sit back down but it still growled at me. Neither the landlady nor I had given the dog a thought during the pie incident. It knew I would take a bundle handed to me by its mistress but when it saw me apparently helping myself to a pie on the bar it thought I was stealing it and reacted accordingly. I was put off of pork pies for quite a long time after that!

Films gave kids the chance to see large animals that live in jungles in far away countries, *Tarzan* films being the best of these. But when the circus came to town, usually Billy Smart's or Chipperfield's, parents would take children to watch the show. The joy, then, was seeing real, live jungle animals; elephants, lions, tigers and other exotic beasts would be paraded around the circus ring.

Circuses set up their tents either on Southampton Common or in Mayflower Park, and when the posters went up in shop windows telling the population that a circus was due soon, excitement was rife. As a butcher's boy, James had a distinct advantage:

Every time a circus came to town, posters went up in a lot of small shops. I was working in Ted Martin's butchers shop and he always displayed a poster in the window. As a thank you for this, the shop owners were always given two free tickets to see the show. Mr Martin wasn't in the least interested in seeing this, so the tickets were passed to me. Then I would collect my best friend Edwin Wheeler and the two of us would go off and sit in our free seats to enjoy the show.

Another popular animal trip was a visit to London Zoo. Children could get to within the width of the bars on the animals' cages and really take a good look at these savage animals from far away lands.

SHOPPING

Two things dominated shopping in the 1950s: early closing on Wednesdays and all-day closing on Sundays. Shops traditionally closed at one o'clock in the afternoons on Wednesdays, so anything not bought by this time had to be gone without. Sundays were a day of rest and for religious worship, so shops were closed for the whole of the day. Families could go to church services together and many children spent the afternoons at Sunday school.

This was the decade when shops finally had stock to sell after the ravages of wartime and rationing – life was returning to normal. For the children growing up in Southampton, that meant new shops, more choice and, of course, running errands! Di Baker remembers a trip to buy some essentials for the family; 'I remember walking up to the corner shop to buy five Woodbines and half a pound of broken biscuits, aged four.' Margaret Hitch (*née* Read), born in 1948 and who lived in Argyle Road, remembers 'going to the Co-op shop for Mum and having to remember the number – 21739.'

Paddy Curran remembers the benefit of running family errands:

With no fridge the food was kept in the larder, which was usually situated on the north side of the house so it was always in the shade. This meant that shopping was a daily ritual and I was often sent on errands. I didn't object because the man at the grocer's often gave me a free sweet.

Dave Wooders remembers what he was expected to do:

We still had ration books for clothing and sweets. I was about eight. I used to do a football *Echo* run and I would go to Bitterne Triangle to Elliot's, a paper shop, and take the newspapers – they used to come in around 6 p.m. I would go up there and queue up and I remember that there were the regulars and there was a woman and we got talking. Of course, my parents couldn't afford sweets, so the sweet ration was no good to us. I used to exchange them with this woman for her clothing coupons. I would give her our sweet coupons. Then, if I needed a new pair of trousers, Mum could save up for them.

Coal was used in houses but it was an expensive means of heating so alternative fuels were looked for. The gas works in Northam was the solution for this in many households, as they had mountains of coke always on hand which was sold at a reasonable price. It was the children's job to go and get this cheap, but very efficient, means of heating. Dave Wooders remembers this errand well:

My father built a little truck. What my youngest sister June and I would have to do on Saturday mornings was push that from Oaktree Road to Northam, just where St Mary's is, and that was where you could get coke. You would have to push that over there and get two bags of coke. The guy over there would load it up and we'd have to push it back. If we did that we'd have the 3d or whatever it was to go to the pictures.

Shirley, as today, was a local shopping Mecca. Brian Stansbridge has a super recollection of the myriad of shops in the area:

Shirley High Street: Home & Colonial; Maypole; Lipton's; Owens and Cozens, the fish and chip shops. Handleys in Romsey Road, where you could buy air guns and knives; Winter & Worth's for school uniform; Woolworths – for everything including those wonderful Airfix soldiers and Christmas presents (flannels for everyone!);

Delbridges or Holden's for pigeon peas (for pea shooters) and bamboo canes (essential to make bows and arrows); Beirne's, the second-hand shop that also sold things like pea shooters and musical instruments. Mr Dear, the tobacconist, Cuff's the hairdresser (who snipped my ear once) and the sweet shop, all in Church Street – lemonade powder (shame of shame – filling our back pockets with sweets whilst the proprietor was distracted); the corner shops – Mr Brown's; Joslin's; Holman's; Denham's (who also operated the local taxi wearing a peaked cap).

Jane Waters remembers other shops in the area:

We shopped at Mr Olden's grocers on the corner of Upper Shirley Avenue and Twyford Avenue. Along that parade there was also Mr Frank Dummer, who had a radio repair shop, Mr Burnett the butcher and the Parker family who ran the newsagent and greengrocer. Our favourite shop was in Bellemoor Road. It was called The Gay Spot and it was a sweet shop. My friend Teresa and I used to go around there and buy lemonade powder and sherbet fountains.

These lists show the sheer variety of businesses operating in a small local area of the city at the time.

FOOD

If families could afford them, Southampton's children could eat hamburgers and fish fingers for the first time, care of Wimpey in 1954 and Birdseye in 1955 respectively. However, often these were treats only to be dreamed of. Di Baker remembers leaner mealtimes; 'There were the days when we only had bread and dripping to eat.'

More often than not, egg and chips or filling suet puddings were staples, with, perhaps, a Sunday roast joint of lamb, pork or beef if they were lucky. Paddy Curran remembers just such meals:

> With the lack of sweets we always ate our dinner, although our diet left a lot to be desired – bread and dripping probably being the worst but we would all fight over who got the jelly that had separated from the fat. Nothing got wasted because if there were any leftovers we would have bubble and squeak, which was just leftovers fried. One thing I will say though is that toast cooked on a coal fire with a toasting fork is the best ever – no toaster can hope to match it. We had a lot of home cooking in the early days when Mum didn't work – favourites were steak and kidney pie and rabbit stew. Rabbit was still in favour in the pre-myxomatosis days.

David Preston remembers how terrified he was when he accidentally caught a large trout in the Itchen. He should have thrown it back. Instead, he took the fish home, looking over his shoulder all the way, expecting to see the police hot on his trail. This didn't happen and he got home safely. The whole family enjoyed a rare meal of fresh trout.

TERRITORY

Another part of growing up was the fierce rivalry where territory was concerned. Many kids believed that shops in their own district were far superior to any in other parts of Southampton, as James remembers:

> One of the best friends I had at Portswood Secondary Modern School lived in the St Denys area of Southampton. This was close

to Portswood where I lived so we spent time in each other's company. Sometimes we were around his area and sometimes in mine. This was fine by us both and we hardly ever had a cross word so friendly were we both to each other. That is, until the day we stopped to buy a bag of chips from the shop just around the corner from the road where he lived. We stopped by the River Itchen to share these between us. He sighed as he ate one, then announced that the shop they came from, Best's Fish and Chip Shop, served the best chips in the whole of Southampton. I stopped in mid-munch at this insult to the chip shop that was in close proximity to my own home, Lock's Fish and Chips. My family and I had bought our chips from this shop for years and there was no doubt in my mind that they held the title of the Best Chips in Southampton. This argument raged on between us over all the rest of the years of our schooldays and was never really resolved. Neither of us was ever prepared to back down on the fact that our own chip shop was the best. In point of fact, both shops were equal in the quality of their chips, it was simply where they were situated that made the difference to both of us.

Magazine advertisements and recipes in the 1950s offer a telling peep into what was on offer to eat and drink. The 4 February 1950 edition of *Woman* devotes a full page to a familiar Cadbury product called Bourn-vita. 'Twice as many people as before the war are getting better sleep and more energy by drinking Bourn-vita,' it claims. It was a snip at only 1s 10d (16p) a tin. Bird's 'three times sure' baking powder would help make cakes and pancakes rise and, just in case families could not obtain enough fruit and vegetables to ensure their toddlers had enough vitamin C, Delrosa rosehip syrup was offered at 1s 9d a bottle – 'doctors recommend it, your chemist stocks it, your children thrive on it.' Tummy upsets were dealt with by Milk of Magnesia, which would bring 'smiles for Mummy ... ', and infants were fed Robinson's Patent Groats, which took one minute to cook to make into gruel.

Vegetables offer an 'adventure in cooking' to the 1950s housewife, eager to gain ideas to feed her family from the garden produce. Recipes for casseroles of rice, cabbage and tomatoes, baked vegetable pie and American parsnip stew sound a little dull to twenty-first-century tastes, but the dishes were livened up by the recommendation to use

Woman magazine was very popular with ladies in the 1950s. Chris Newman's mother, Nina, enjoyed reading it. (Image courtesy of Chris Newman)

a 'corrugated vegetable cutter, vegetable ball makers and an apple corer to add variety and interest to vegetable dishes.'

The 1950 February 25th edition of the magazine offers Heinz strained foods for babies. The persuasive advertising blurb tells mothers that the machinery used to make the foods has been 'designed and built to produce baby foods – and nothing else.' The company offered fourteen varieties of foods, all offering 'true, fresh flavours.'

Hovis bread, bigger size Mars Bars ('For the 3 out of 4 who want more for their 2 points' – sweet rationing was still in place in 1950), Libby's Evaporated Milk and Marmite, 'For better cooking EVERY day' all have substantial advertisements. Meanwhile, every mother knows that Bovril 'Prevents that sinking feeling' at eleven o'clock when you are 'half-way between the breakfast you didn't have time for and the dinner you haven't started ... ' Not only is a look at advertising of the period informative, it also reveals just how little our tastes have changed in the intervening years.

FAMILY LIFE

For many 1950s families, outside toilets, tin baths in the kitchen, very cold houses, the front-door key on a string behind the letterbox and chickens and/or pigs in the garden were a matter of course. Life was enlivened by visits from the milk man, the rag and bone man, with his familiar cry of 'RAG Boooone' and the ability to cart off unwanted items, and the knife grinder.

Di Baker has a vivid memory of being three years of age; 'Because my Mother was terrified of spiders, I had to put on my wellies and go down into the coal cellar to put money into the gas meter.' Money being tight, she also remembers the loss of the family joint one day. This anecdote also sheds more light on what feeding the gas meter entailed:

> Up until 1952 we rented in Wynn Road in Portswood, in a large old house that had been divided into flats. We lived on the ground floor. The place was infested with rats that mainly lived in the coal cellars and tried to keep out of sight of the owls that inhabited the large trees in the garden. One day, when funds were available, Mum got a beef roast to cook for tea. She left it on an enamel plate on the table in the kitchen while we were in the living room. Suddenly, there was a crash and Mum and I rushed into the kitchen to see the plate on the floor and the last side of the meat disappearing through the large hole in the skirting board. I think that my mother still has the plate!

CLOTHES

Girls wore hair ribbons and short socks, with dresses and cardigans. Boys resembled miniature versions of their fathers, often wearing ties, but with bands of elastic holding up their long socks. However, men wore long trousers and boys wore shorts until they were at least twelve years old. James remembers the joys, and otherwise, of wearing them:

> In summer short trousers came into their own. It was more comfortable to have bare legs, socks rolled down to ankles and sandals instead of shoes. You could go paddling in streams and rivers and, as long as the water didn't come over your knees, your trousers stayed dry. In winter, however, things were very different. In fierce winds and freezing cold days the shorts were our enemies and the worst example of this was sore knees, caused by the trousers rubbing against the sides of your knees as you walked. Boy's short trousers had a linen lining that stopped just about two inches from the bottom of the legs. It was this rough stretch of unprotected material that rubbed your knees sore as the cold took hold. It meant nightly sessions with our mothers, as they rubbed Vaseline into the affected areas. I don't know which was worse, the soreness from the trousers or the agony of the Vaseline.

Boys wore short trousers until they were twelve years old – summer and winter. (Image taken at Milestones Museum, courtesy of Hampshire County Council Museums and Archives Service)

Sue Diaper, who always had a new dress at Easter, had some of her clothes made for her by a dressmaker family friend.

Sue Diaper and her little brother John in 1959, in Mays department store. Sue is wearing her favourite dress, made by a local dressmaker. Mays was the old department store, which became Owen Owen and is now a £1 shop. Sue's mother took her and her brother to the photographer at the store to have the photograph taken. (Image courtesy of Sue Diaper)

Sue Diaper loved her red polka dot dress, just visible beneath her white cardigan as she looks at the camera in this 1956 photograph, taken at Butlins. (Image courtesy of Sue Diaper)

I remember her making me some lovely dresses. One of my favourites was white with tiny red polka dots. It had puffed sleeves and a lovely full skirt. I loved it. Another one was white organza with a pale pink lining. It was really pretty but a bit scratchy. Another one was white with a pink underskirt with a pink ribbon round the waist. I used to have long hair and when I was younger usually had it in plaits and sometimes the plaits were put up on my head. I always wore ribbon. Another dress I remember was my first 'grown-up' dress. It was black and white check with three-quarter sleeves and a white collar and it had a lovely organdie petticoat underneath which made it stand out a little. I remember being invited to a friend's birthday party just before Christmas and we must have been about ten. She was a girl I went to school with and she lived in Bevois Street. I didn't have anything to wear so Mum took me to Frasers in St Mary Street and bought me a really lovely blue party dress with some black suede shoes. Looking back, I've got no idea how she afforded it, but she was determined I was going to the party in a pretty dress.

DISCIPLINE

Parental discipline was something that all kids had to endure. Parents dealt with misdemeanours with smacks and sometimes children were sent to bed early without any supper. At school, it was the cane that solved behaviour problems and the majority of boys did not complete his education without feeling the sting from the cane over the back of his hands. The smarting weals left by the cane were often badges of pride in the playground afterwards.

Kids were told who they could trust in times of trouble, such as getting separated from parents while out on shopping trips. You could trust a policeman, a doctor, a shop assistant, a nurse etc. Child abusers, although certainly a part of society, were not mentioned. Rules were instilled into every child, as was the warning 'Never accept sweets or rides from a stranger.'

James remembers one particular day when this warning sounded loud and clear:

> I was walking home one day and was in my own road when a lorry appeared and slowed up. A man I had never seen before leaned out of the cab and shouted to me. 'Come on nipper, jump up here and ride the rest of your way home.' The warnings my mother had always drummed into us about accepting rides from strangers immediately set bells ringing so I started to run for the safety of my home. But the lorry quickly caught me up and, turning in fear, I was delighted to see that the man behind the wheel was my own father. The man I didn't know was his mate who was sitting on the passenger's side of the cab. My dad now beckoned me and I broke the speed limit as I rushed up and jumped into the cab. I got a ride home and a pat on the back from my dad for doing the right thing when I didn't recognise someone who was offering me a lift.

Boys and girls learned discipline at home, at school and in the streets, where bad behaviour attracted punishment, usually a clip around the ear from passing police officers. Discipline (and fun) also came from joining youth organisations. Mike Holloway joined 12th Southampton St Mark's Cub Pack, which was the start of his membership of the Boy Scout Movement up to 1961, progressing through the ranks from Cub to Assistant Scoutmaster (ASM) with the 21st Romsey, Nursling and Rownhams group. He was in the scout party that attended the 8th World Scout Jamboree, The New Horizons Jamboree at Niagara-on-the-Lake, Ontario in Canada, in 1954. The criteria for this were that he be over fourteen years of age and had attained his First Class Badge.

Mike Holloway was selected to go to the 8th World Scout Jamboree in Canada in 1954. (Picture courtesy of the *Southern Daily Echo*)

His parents received sponsorship of £50 towards the £130 cost of this prestigious trip, and Mike had to raise the £10 pocket money he would need and also contribute towards the outstanding cost of the trip. He did this by getting a paper round, which he remembers to this day:

I remember that paper round well. Six days a week with approximately 100 deliveries in just Paynes and Waterloo Roads. In those days, the weekly magazines were included. Friday was the heaviest because it included the *Radio Times*. There was no point in using a bike because the papers went into most of the houses. The newsagent was Bert Prowting, whose shop was in Park Road. Permains Bakery, also in Park Road, was the last delivery where I often bought a freshly baked loaf to take home.

On 12 August 1955, the five senior scouts, Laurie Watkins (Itchen Division), Paul Diggle and Mervyn Hamlyn (Central Division) and Barry Herbert and Mike Holloway (West Division) set off from Southampton Central Station. In the days when long-haul flights were still in the future, there were three refuelling stops:

> On arrival, somewhat jet-lagged and disoriented, we were taken to a separate arrivals lounge and were introduced to Canadian families who gave us splendid hospitality for a few days before sailing across Lake Ontario to Niagara-on-the-Lake for the Jamboree.

The Jamboree's opening ceremony was very formal with contingents from each company marching to their allocated positions in the arena. Lady Baden-Powell attended.

On 12 August 1955, the five senior scouts, Laurie Watkins (Itchen Division), Paul Diggle and Mervyn Hamlyn (Central Division) and Barry Herbert and Mike Holloway (West division) set off for the 8th World Scout Jamboree from Southampton Central Station. (Image courtesy of Mike Holloway)

The Jamboree's opening ceremony was very formal with contingents from each company marching to their allocated positions in the arena. Lady Baden-Powell attended. (Image courtesy of Mike Holloway)

There were outings to Niagara Falls, both the Canadian side and the USA side. We were taken on a tour of the Ontario Hydro Power Station, which uses the flow of water from Lake Erie to Lake Ontario. There were swimming parties to Lake Ontario.

No campfires were allowed on the Jamboree site, so all cooking was done on home-made charcoal burning stoves. Ours were made from 5-gallon oil drums.

The toilets (latrines) were in bell tents distributed throughout the Jamboree site. The equivalent of a WC consisted of back-to-back wooden box units with two seats. These were placed over very deep holes previously dug by giant screw bits. The urinals were also simple with a funnel attached to a pipe placed over a third deep hole. I have no idea how these toilets were kept clean but they were always in good condition. I also have no idea what facilities were available for ladies.

The day of departure for our homeward journey was not without incident; whilst waiting at the airport we were informed that our plane was delayed at New York due to radio problems. When we were finally seated on the plane, a truck attending the aircraft managed to hit one of the propellers, so it was off the plane to be told that there would be a delay until the next day. That was fine by us spending another day with our wonderful Canadian hosts but the problem was letting our families at home know of the delay. Not many homes had telephones in those days, so once the message got back to Southampton various people were sent out to each family with the information of the twenty-four-hour delay.

Brian Stansbridge was a member of 2nd Southampton Scouts:

I was in the cubs and enjoyed it and was exposed to all the iconic aspects of scouting, but it lost its attraction by the time I was old enough for Scouts. Maybe there was something a little ridiculous about all the 'Dyb Dyb Dyb, Dob Dob Dob' ritual and so on. Also, we only ever seemed to go to camp in huts in the New Forest. I wanted to go under canvas and build wash-stands out of sticks.

There was no doubt that scouting was an important part of growing up for many children in Southampton. Scouting's Golden

Brian Stansbridge was an enthusiastic cub scout. (Image courtesy of Brian Stansbridge)

Gill Holloway poses proudly in her Girl Guide uniform in 1952. (Photo courtesy Gill Holloway)

Jubilee was celebrated on 24 May 1958, with a pageant of Scouts and Girl Guides at the Southampton Speedway Stadium.

Many of the experiences detailed in this book have been concerned with boys' toys, games and having fun. However, girls joined in and took advantage of opportunities, particularly in organisations such as the Girl Guides. When she was ten, Gill Holloway (née Haskell), born in October 1939, was a Girl Guide. She remembers what she got up to with the other girls:

The Church of the Ascension in Bitterne Park had a Girl Guide Company, which met in the Church House. Once a month, we attended Church Parade where six Guides were chosen for the colour party. I progressed to leader of a patrol and often carried the colours at Church Parade. At the weekly meetings we learned how to tie knots, prepare for badges, enjoy competitions between patrols, of which I recall we had a limited time to collect a list of ten items e.g. two pence bus ticket, an oak leaf, etc. The complete company of young girls would be scouring the area of Bullar Road and The Triangle back in the days of minimal traffic.

When Gillian was thirteen she joined the Sea Rangers. This was the girls' version of the Sea Scouts.

On leaving the Girl Guides I joined the Sea Ranger crew of Sea Ranger Ship Southampton, which had its own meeting hut off Broadlands Road in Bassett. For a regatta, many Ranger crews gathered in Gosport where we lived on board TS *Foudroyant*. She was an amazing old ship, a bit like the *Victory*. The long dining benches were stacked away at night so we could sling our hammocks.

The Sea Ranger crew of Sea Ranger Ship Southampton in 1954. (Photo courtesy Gill Holloway)

TS *Foudroyant*, at Gosport in 1954. This was used for accommodation during regattas. Sea Rangers would sling their hammocks below decks. (Photo courtesy Gill Holloway)

Mike Holloway remembers the co-operation between the Scouting and the Girl Guide movements – and also reminds us that the age of chivalry was not quite dead in 1950s Southampton:

> It was at a Girl Guide function at the Central Hall where we met Lady Baden Powell in the mid-fifties.
>
> I was a Senior Scout with the 12th Southampton St Marks. Our Senior Scout Master was Frank Cox and someone in the Southampton Guide Association had approached him requesting some Senior Scouts to assist at the function. The approach to the front of the Central Hall was up a flight of steps quite different to how it is now. Some Guides were expected to arrive on their

bicycles and our job was to carry the bicycles up the steps and inside the main doors of the entrance.

We had been instructed to wear our uniforms. We were standing informally by the doors at the top of the steps when a car arrived. The host Guiders greeted the car and out stepped Lady Olave Baden Powell. She walked up the steps to us and shook hands with all of us. She was probably surprised to see Senior Scouts at a Guide function. I recall her asking, 'What are you boys doing here?' So we told her that we had been asked to carry the Guides' bikes up the steps.

Joining these organisations, and others such as the Sea Cadets, was good training for the time when a boy's call-up papers came through the letterbox of their homes. James was not a member of these organisations and so paid out for his non-participation:

I wasn't in the least tempted to join the Scouts or any other organisation as a boy, so I was completely unprepared for the harsh discipline that was dished out on a daily basis at the Vindicatrix Sea Training School in Sharpness. I had to grow up quickly there if I hoped to pass the six-week course and from there go to sea in Britain's Merchant Navy. I was there in one of the coldest winters I can remember – February 1957. I always say I missed National Service but in getting through that course, then serving aboard various ships sailing in and out of Southampton, I think, though, I went through everything anyone in any of the three services did. It made a man of me and I will always be grateful for that.

THE ARRIVAL OF TELEVISION

Television arrived for James in 1957. Many working-class families had discovered that TV sets could be rented far cheaper than the price of buying one (a tabletop Pye 51 was 51 guineas and the Valradio Limited flat screen projection television was £148, at a time when the average annual salary was just over £100). Once the rental shop was contacted, they did the rest. A small screen, black and white set was delivered and an aerial placed on the roof of the house concerned, and it was in this way that television arrived for the masses. James remembers:

> That year I was away at sea most of the time, serving on the Union Castle lines' *Winchester Castle*. When I went into our home after paying off from the ship I was proudly shown the TV sitting on the top of Mum's sideboard. We had arrived and the posh people of our neighbourhood had nothing on us anymore!

Dave Wooders' family bought their television:

> The only reason we had television was because my Gran sold her bungalow in Thornhill and came to live with us. Half the money went to Mum and half went to her brother. We could then afford a TV. We had lived with her when we were bombed out and we stayed with her for a while until we got another place. I was thirteen or fourteen when Gran came to stay.

Mike Holloway, born in 1939, says, 'The first time I saw television was December 1954 in London on a Sunday afternoon. It was a very early hook-up with TV in Europe showing a football match between Italy and another country. It was fascinating.'

Until 1955, the BBC was the only television broadcaster in the UK. This monopoly was shattered on 22 September, when commercial television burst on to the screen with its headline programme, ATV's *Sunday Night at the London Palladium*. The first advertisement on television, for Gibbs SR toothpaste, underwhelmed many, as advertising was felt to be vulgar. The BBC did not carry advertisements as the licence payer funded it (the first combined radio and television licence was issued in 1946 and cost £2). By 1957, broadcasting to schools was underway, thanks to Associated-Rediffusion.

THE KING IS DEAD

In 1952, the ailing King George VI had waved goodbye to his eldest daughter Princess Elizabeth, accompanied by her husband Prince Philip, as she embarked on a tour of the Commonwealth. This was a tour the King had not been well enough to undertake himself, having undergone a lung operation just weeks before. The King, worn out by successive worries, had taken his doctor's advice and stayed at home. It was the last time they were to see each other. On 6 February 1952, the King died in his sleep and Great Britain, its fading Empire and the Commonwealth had a new queen.

The *Guardian*, on Thursday, 7 February 1952, reported: 'The news of the sudden death at Sandringham of King George VI was received by the nation with profound sorrow. The announcement from Sandringham at 10.45 yesterday morning said: "The King, who retired to rest last night in his usual health, passed peacefully away in his sleep early this morning."'

Rod Andrews remembers his confusion at the King's death; 'I can recall bumping into a neighbour's child who stunned us (and puzzled me) with his news. "The king is dead! And our new king is going to be a queen!"'

Tony Caws also remembers the end of the George VI era:

I remember walking down East Street one lunchtime and, at the top of the street, buying a single sheet published quickly by, I believe, the *Daily Echo* concerning the King's death. I think that

I paid about 1d or perhaps 2d for it. I read it while walking down East Street and, having read it, selling it for the princely sum of a tanner [6d] to a man who had heard of the King's death and desperately wanted the sheet that I had.

The BBC reported that, 'As the news of the King's death spread, all cinemas and theatres closed, and BBC programmes were cancelled except for news bulletins. Flags in every town were at half-mast, and sports fixtures were cancelled.'

King George VI had been a popular monarch and the nation was genuinely sorry to lose him. Their new queen was very young and most felt sorry that she had no time to grieve for her father before duty intervened.

The coronation of a British monarch was televised for the first time when BBC cameras were set up to record that of Queen Elizabeth II in Westminster Abbey in 1953. Television was still very much a novelty that only the rich could afford. However, many households obtained their first television set to be able to watch the Coronation. Whole families (and often their neighbours down the street) gathered around the wooden boxes holding the screens to see Her Majesty Queen Elizabeth II crowned.

Mike Holloway remembers the Coronation:

I can remember sitting with my mother and listening to the commentary on the radio on Coronation Day. We did not own one of those early television sets. Part of the Coronation celebrations was the firing of a chain of Bonfire Beacons around the British Isles. The Southampton bonfire was on the common on land just north of 'The Flats', or football pitches. Wood was brought in from all over the town and it was the job of the scouts to build the bonfire. It must have been thirty feet high and in the shape of a tall thin pyramid. The base had a hollow chamber for the kindling fuel to be placed at the last minute. Once construction was underway, it became necessary for the bonfire to be guarded against unauthorised lighting. I was never involved in any of the guard duty but a friend told of one night when some young men attempted to light the fire. The guards outnumbered the attackers and the police were called as a precaution, but it all ended peacefully.

James's memories of Queen Elizabeth II's Coronation sum up the mood of the time:

The Queen's Coronation in 1953 was such a big event that whole roads were decorated for it and street parties were arranged all over the country. In my case this was Belgrave Road and the grown-ups did a wonderful job of making it look like a fairy grotto for this huge and important event. Flags and bunting were flying across the road, fixed between the houses, and small flags abounded everywhere. At school, we were all given a Coronation mug that I proudly carried home and gave to my mother.

The Coronation was shown for the first time on television and those people posh enough to have one of these that year were able to watch as the new queen was crowned. We had to wait a few days

All children were presented with either a china or glass souvenir Coronation mug.

before the whole school was taken to a local cinema so that we could all watch the Coronation on *Pathé News*. I will always remember how proud and thrilled I was as that beautiful crown was placed on the head of Queen Elizabeth, and later, as she went back to Buckingham Palace in that incredible gold coach. We may have been in a cinema watching this but every child there that day cheered as loud as possible, so that our queen would know how proud we all were of her.

Of course, souvenirs were produced en masse. Schoolchildren were each given a Coronation mug in either china or blue glass. Kay Rowe still remembers being presented with hers.

Many souvenirs were produced for the Coronation of Queen Elizabeth II. This one showed the royal procession as the illustration was wound through the casing. (Image taken at Milestones Museum, courtesy of Hampshire County Council Museums and Archives Service)

We lived in Cossack Green and we had the street party in the square opposite my house. There were lots of children and all the mums put on a lovely spread of sandwiches, cakes, biscuits and I think there was jelly. After the party, we were all taken to the local church hall and we were presented with a bag of goodies and the boxed blue glass mug. Although I was only six years old, I remember what a lovely day I had.

Even toys remembered the momentous event – the Coronation procession was immortalised on paper in a tin-plate toy frame with a handle at either end. Turning the handles scrolled the paper through the frame and the procession proceeded.

CHRISTMAS

The excitement of Christmas started long before the big day, when homemade decorations were eagerly made from tin-foil cake cases and gummed strips of coloured paper. As was tradition, holly was brought indoors to help brighten the home and fir trees were cut down to be hung with glittering baubles or were purchased from Kingsland Market. Shopping in Southampton was an exciting affair. From about four o'clock in the afternoon the shops were lit up and shop windows were crowded with toys.

In some cases, Christmas brought unbelievable luxury and joy as dreams came true early in the morning of 25 December. Boys were delighted if they found Meccano sets, or other building toys such as Bayko, in their stockings. But, as girls thrilled to receive dolls, dolls houses and prams, skipping ropes and other feminine things, it was a boy's dream to wake up and find a train set on the end of his bed. In the 1950s these were mainly clockwork, although some were electric, with a set of tracks that went round in a circle, and the engine and carriages, round and round continuously. It sounds boring now to spend so much time watching these trains simply going round in a circle, but at the time, young boys revelled in it.

Paddy Curran remembers Christmas:

> I didn't have much in the way of toys, although I do remember a fireman that climbed a ladder, and a six shooter with a barrel that went round and 'real' bullets that you loaded (I was especially proud of that gun). I had a few Dinky toys but my real *big* present was when I came down one year on Christmas morning to find an electric train set. It was a simple set, a round track, one engine and three trucks but I played with it constantly. I made a bridge for the train to go under and our budgie delighted us by perching on the engine as it went round, and hopping off just before the tunnel, before running around and rejoining on the other side.

Chris Newman remembers the Christmas Day he became 'Stirling Chris':

> My dad was very naturally skilled with his hands and would design and make things. He decided he could design and construct a peddle car for his only nipper. I couldn't believe my eyes when, freshly painted in blue, it was wheeled into the room on Christmas day. These contraptions were sometimes known collectively as 'Noddy cars'. But I can tell you I wouldn't have swapped mine for Noddy's – even though I had to peddle it to get anywhere. It was superb. It had all sorts of gadgets – horn, handbrake, steering wheel – I literally wore it out.

'Stirling Chris', c. 1958. Chris Newman's father built his beloved peddle car, which he literally wore out with use. Chris called it the Bluebird as it was painted blue. (Image courtesy of Chris Newman)

Many companies held Christmas parties for staff and their children. These were very popular and are remembered with smiles and much nostalgia. Di Baker was one of the lucky guests:

> My father worked in the docks for Harland & Wolff. Every Christmas they would have a party for their workers' children in the Territorial Army Hall in Carlton Place. I think that I first went when I was four and I had to look after my two younger cousins and make sure they got their share of any goodies. We had sandwiches cut in to triangles (as a change from the rectangular ones we had every day), jelly, small cakes and a piece of Christmas cake. As we left they gave each of us an orange and 2s (10p).

Chris Newman remembers the joys of the Christmas parties on the Ford site in Swaythling; 'They always did a really good children's party.'

Christmas was a time for family parties and music. Chris Newman remembers his Uncle Steve building a puppet theatre in his Aunt Ethel's home in Spring Road, in about 1958, when he was six. The puppeteers, his cousins Michael and June, put their heads through holes in the curtain and became part of the entertainment. His musician father also enthusiastically joined in the family Christmas celebrations.

Christmas was a special time for kids. Chris Newman is on the left of the main table, fifth from the camera at the Briggs Motor Company party, now part of Ford. (Image courtesy of Chris Newman)

Dad locked himself in the shed like a mad inventor and you could hear 'Pow! Pow! Pow!' He brought out a scaled down, upright double bass he'd made just before Christmas. He also made a washboard and played 'My Old Man's a Dustman.'

Myron Sowtus' family loved getting together to enjoy music. Each of his four uncles and five aunts played an instrument – violin, accordion, drums, even the Jew's harp – and the young Myron

Often parties meant film shows, eagerly watched. Chris Newman is the lad to the right, on a chair by himself. His rapt face tells all! (Image courtesy of Chris Newman)

drove his Aunt Clare mad by repeatedly asking her to play Russ Conway's 'Sidesaddle' on her violin! What comes across is a sense of the 1950s family making its own entertainment and thoroughly enjoying themselves in the bargain!

All of the make-do meals eaten by so many during the year were eclipsed on Christmas Day, when delicacies like turkey or chicken were served with vegetables and placed in front of children whose eyes opened wide in wonder. It was a special meal. And afterwards, there was Christmas pudding.

Paddy Curran remembers his Christmas meal:

> We only had chicken at Christmas, probably because it was too expensive. Then my mum would make the puddings and we all had a stir. When it was dished up you all hoped to get one of the silver 3d bits that were stirred into the mixture.

Chris Newman remembers Christmas pudding, the recipe which is still used in his family today; 'This was made with loads of brandy, rum and stout included in the traditional pre-Christmas pudding stir. It was a greatly anticipated annual ritual.'

Family life was not all rosy. Some children had to endure hardship or lived in fear of bullying family members. Others were under constant scrutiny, even after the war was over. For example, many Polish people came to England to escape the atrocities during the war and Myron Sowtus's father was among these. Myron remembers the police interviews his father had to attend, even into the 1950s:

As my father was Polish he had to attend Portswood Police Station every so often for an interview. Some years later, I learned from my mother that on one occasion my father took me with him to the station. During the interview, he was asked what newspaper he read and after he answered this was then asked if there were any other papers he read (the implication here being communist literature) to which my father said, 'No.' It was then that I apparently said, 'Yes you do.' I can imagine the expression on my father's face, and the policeman, with sudden interest, said, 'Do you know which one, Son?' To which I replied, 'The *Beano*.'

Rod Andrews sums up the family in the 1950s:

I had one loving mum and one loving dad, who was still recovering from being a POW in the Second World War. I had one sister who was six years older than me. We lived in a rented house, my dad returned to work as a labourer with the Borough Engineers Depot. Money was tight, of course, but I had half of what I wanted and everything I probably needed. I was never aware of going without. I had regular and well nourished meals, a warm bed and some toys and, above all, I had love.

seven

TRAINS, PLANES AND AUTOMOBILES

The 1950s was a decade of much change. The Second World War was pivotal to all that came immediately afterwards, and its effects were being slowly tackled. Bombsites were cleared, new houses were constructed and people rebuilt their lives. Prosperity was slow in coming but there were buds of a new world emerging from the war-ravaged doldrums.

True, it was still a common sight to see the rag and bone man, the milkman and the street cleaners all with horses and carts, and the 'by-products' of these working street animals were eagerly sought after, as Janet Bowen remembers:

As my dad had poor health after the war, he worked on a road-sweeping gang, which consisted of the men and a horse and cart. These were stabled at the top of Radstock Road, the Cranbury Road end. Every day after school, I had to meet Dad with a homemade trolley to bring the horse's manure back for the garden.

Janet Bowen's charming drawing tells all – you can guess where she ended up! (Image courtesy of Janet Bowen)

This particular Monday, Mum had left the washing rinse water in the bathtub for Dad to use to water the garden. Backing out of the yard gate, my calves touched the edge of the bath and I fell back into the cold water. Mum had spent the day washing and was rather angry to have more wet clothes to dry! Having to go indoors to change, I was late meeting Dad; he also was cross with me! What a day!

If the horse's owner did not want the manure, kids were tuned into this natural fertilizer and would follow horses as they worked from street to street. Once the horse answered the call of nature the following children swooped and shovelled the manure into the buckets they were carrying. This was sold to relatives and neighbours and the pocket money gained was often spent on sweets.

BICYCLES

Janet Bowen remembers her father building her an ASP (All Spare Parts) bicycle for riding to school.

Janet Bowen and her 'All Spare Parts' bike, c. 1951. It did not last long and she was soon walking to school again! (Image courtesy of Janet Bowen)

> I remember Dad making me an ASP bike to get to school. It didn't last
> long as it broke where the handlebars went into the frame. So then
> I was back to walking the mile-plus to Itchen Grammar School each day.

The only school run in those days was when children were late and had to hurry to get to school on time!

MOTORBIKES

Motorbikes were the in-thing for the modern teenager in the 1950s and many parents agonised when their child managed to get their hands on one.

Gill Holloway perched on her dad's motorbike, c. 1951. (Image courtesy of Gill Holloway)

Dave Wooders remembers his with pride:

When I was a bellboy at sea I made enough money from Southampton to New York and back to buy a brand new motorbike. I couldn't believe it! You had to look good – the hands, the cuffs, the hair – and the Americans just threw money at you so long as you were polite. You know what Americans are like – I'm not running them down. 'Give the bellboy a tip.' 'OK.' One would give you two dollars but the one behind would give you five.

Teddy Boys were known for their motorbikes as well as their exaggerated clothing. To have a 500cc Norton was a status symbol because these were very big and powerful bikes. Teddy Boys were inspired to ride bikes like this because they saw Marlon Brando doing just that, as the head of an American Harley Davidson motorcycle gang in the very popular film *The Wild One*, which came out in 1953. In his leathers and riding his Harley, Brando quickly became an idol of Teddy Boys in England. Easy payment finance for young people was the key, and speeding in excess of 100 miles an hour on Britain's improving roads gave these riders their nickname: Ton-up Boys. They frequented the many transport cafés along the way and turned them into bases from where road races took place. The popular bike for these was the Triton Café Racer. This bike was made for speed with a Triumph twin motorcycle engine and a Norton feathered frame. They were popular from the end of the 1950s onwards. Sadly, for so many young people in the 1950s, motorcycling was out of the question as the most they could afford was a brand new bicycle, on the hire purchase, of course.

BUSES

A beautiful part of Southampton was the Rose Garden that stood opposite the Civic Centre. This had a fountain in the middle, which was lit up at night. The gardens were a noted feature of the city and had stood before the Civic Centre since June 1934. Behind them was the bus station for Hants and Dorset Buses. They gave a service that went beyond Southampton's borders, in their green and yellow livery.

Hants and Dorset Buses owed their existence to the Bournemouth and District Motor Services Ltd, which came into being on 17 March 1916. This was itself part of the larger British Automobile Traction Company, which was part of the British Electrical Traction Company. The new business had big dreams and expansion was rapid. By 1920 it had routes in most of the surrounding countryside and was working its way east. When it

Southampton's Rose Garden, outside the Civic Centre in 1950. (Image courtesy of Julie Green)

took over an existing Southampton company, Trade Cars Ltd – which was based in Shirley and had been set up in 1918 by a keen early driver and prominent local councillor, S. Tebbutt – it decided to change its name to avoid upsetting the locals of the town. The Bournemouth and District Motor Services Company became the Hants and Dorset Motor Services Ltd on 27 July 1920.

The company's bus station was, by 1955, very busy and very congested. Buses in the 1950s were bigger than their earlier counterparts, and having to negotiate between Windsor Terrace and Birmingham Street was no easy feat, particularly when the yard was full. They were both eventually demolished to ease the congestion.

Brian Stansbridge remembers visiting family at Woodlands, Burridge, Bartley, Redbridge and Ashurst, and travelling on Hants and Dorset buses to do so:

I remember the thick cardboard tickets and the clipping machines; feeling travel sick and being held by Dad on the rear platform to 'get some air' as the bus hurtled along and wondering what the little advertisements with 'This site could be selling for you' on them meant. It sounded like a threat of some kind.

The red buses, run by Southampton Corporation Transport and based at the bus depots in Portswood and Shirley, covered all the areas within Southampton. The Corporation had experimented unsuccessfully with motorbuses before they finally caught on with the public in 1919. The first motorbus route was from St James' Road to the Clock Tower and was launched on 31 July of that year. More routes soon followed, aided by the acquisition of Northam Bridge in 1929 and the Floating Bridge and Roads Company in 1934.

The 1950s were the era of the Guy Motors Arab buses. Guy Motors Ltd had been in business since 1914, founded by Sydney Slater Guy, and had been successfully building buses and military vehicles ever since. The Arab chassis dated from 1933 and in several versions was its most popular bus. It had taken over from the trams that were taken out of service in 1948. It was some years though before the tram lines over which the trams had travelled were dug up. Many a cyclist was late for work because the wheels of their bike had become stuck in the tramlines!

Buses in the fifties in Southampton were rear platform double-deckers. They were exciting to ride on and extremely comfortable after the rough wooden seating of the trams. The windows were set up high and small children had a job trying to look out of them at the passing streets. For this reason, the best seats, the most popular with children, were the two at the very front upstairs. From these seats, children could see right ahead while pretending that they were driving the bus. The conductor would come upstairs every time more people got on and give his immortal cry, 'Any more fares, please?'

A Guy Arab bus – well remembered by those who grew up in the 1950s.
(Image courtesy of Tom Lingwood and the Southampton and District
Transport Heritage Trust)

The conductors had a ticket machine that they wore at their
waist, suspended from straps over their shoulders. The tickets
were dispensed by pressing tabs on the front, and then the
machine would spill out the required number of tickets for the
fare paid. In the 1950s, this was a matter of just a few pennies.
Some Southampton children began collecting bus tickets, as
others would collect stamps or cigarette cards. Di Baker was
particularly drawn to collecting purple ones!

Older boys used the back platform to show off their manly
status. Once the bus was headed for their stop they would get
up and stand with their back to the road and lean outward, just
stopping themselves from falling off the bus by holding on to the
centre rod. This was meant to impress girls, but there seem to be
no records of it having worked in this direction!

Paddy Curran remembers his bus trips to school:

We didn't have a car so our usual mode of transport was the bus. I would get a bus to school from the age of seven. If we were lucky, we would get the nice conductor who would let us keep our money. We would then spend it on sweets in the little shop that used to be opposite St James' Church.

Eassons' first bus service was from Butts Road to the Floating Bridge, in 1920. The current premises, in Wodehouse Road in Sholing, were built in 1948, on the site of the former garage beside the Easson family home. They went on to offer coach services too, which, unlike their bus routes, have survived into the twenty-first century.

Eassons Coaches ran evening tours in the 1950s. Janet Bowen enjoyed them with her family – her eldest brother and his girlfriend, her mother, a friend, Janet aged sixteen, and her young niece from Trowbridge in front. (Image courtesy of Janet Bowen)

Janet Bowen remembers family trips on the coach fondly:

> We would go to shows by coach on evening trips to Bournemouth and Portsmouth and coach trips to London to see a show. A local coach firm, Eassons, did evening mystery tours and we went on these quite often. We also went to Trowbridge in Wiltshire to visit family. I remember on one occasion going with my eldest brother. We had to change at Salisbury on this journey and I was too scared to go to the toilet on my own, thinking I would be OK till I reached Trowbridge. Well, how I got to my sister's I do not know as there was a walk to her home from the bus, but I know I nearly collapsed when I did get there!

Myron Sowtus, who attended St Mary's College, remembers the school taking advantage of coach trips too:

> [The school] had various Societies, such as the Historical or Geographical, which meant for a small sum you could join and at weekends, normally a Saturday, go on a coach trip to various venues, such as the Roman Baths in Bath or see the Bluebell Railway line and have a ride on the train.

FLOATING BRIDGES

Corporation Transport also operated the two floating bridges that crossed the River Itchen at Woolston and made it possible for traffic and passengers to cross over to Woolston and beyond.

In 1836, the centuries-old crossing operated by the ferrymen from Itchen Ferry Village was put out of business by the floating bridge. It was the brainchild of celebrated civil engineer James Meadows Rendel (1799–1856). He built on previous ideas

The Floating Bridge, June 1957. (Image courtesy of Brenda Buchman, *née* Reader, and Debbie and Tony Deacon)

stretching back centuries and had built such bridges before, namely on the Dart at Dartmouth and on the Tamar between Torpoint and Saltash. The bridge was, essentially, a steam-powered chain-link ferry, originally with one car. It used a pair of chains to draw the car from one side of the river to the other and to stop it being washed downstream by the highly charged current of the River Itchen. However, a second set of chains was added in 1881 to allow two cars to criss-cross the river simultaneously in about four minutes. Between 1878 and 1887 cables replaced the chains. Over time, as technology advanced, diesel bus engines replaced the steam-powered ones. By the 1950s, the wear and tear on the cars was taking its toll and the late 1950s saw the cars regularly out of service – the long-awaited Itchen Bridge could not come soon enough.

The service was free for foot passengers, but a small fee was charged for cars and lorries. Each car had a wide ramp at both ends where people boarded and left the bridge when it arrived at its destination. These were operated by hand cranks and they had a gate across them that was closed when the floating bridge was about to start. Built for strength and longevity, there was certainly no comfort on the floating bridge but passengers could shelter from the rain in the small cabins on either side of the main vehicle platform in the middle.

Many stories have been told of people who were already late for work running down to the river's edge as the floating bridge, with the gate now closed across the loading ramp, starting to pull away. In desperation, some of these leapt across the widening stretch of water hoping to land on the ramp and be let on board for the crossing. Sadly, many didn't make it and landed in the water instead. This, of course, made them even later for work as they now had to go home and change. Buses were always waiting on the Southampton side to take many of the foot passengers on to their destinations.

Di Baker remembers going back and forth on the floating bridge several times 'just for the fun of it!' This was also the case for Janet Bowen:

> I had two half-sisters and a half-brother who all had children. It was my brother's and my job to amuse the younger ones and we would walk to the floating bridge and ride back and fore as many times as we wanted, as pedestrians went free!

The floating bridge became increasingly unable to cope with the amount of traffic it was expected to carry and was replaced by the Itchen Toll Bridge in 1977.

STEAM RAILWAYS

Sue Diaper's feelings on the subject of steam engines echo that of many of Southampton's 1950s children:

> There was a level crossing with a bridge just down the road from Ascupart Junior School and we all used to love waiting on the bridge for the steam train to go under it and we would all disappear in the smoke. I used to love the smell of the smoke.

The steam engine was so popular its complete demise has not been allowed to happen. Instead, it has gained a place in history. Preservation societies and lines dot the country and, in the twenty-first century, the advertised presence of a steam engine is guaranteed to bring crowds to see it send smoke up into the air and to hear the unmistakable sound of the whistle as it rends the air. A ride on a steam engine today is as much of an event as children thought it to be in the fifties.

Growing up in 1950s Southampton presented many children with the enjoyment of train spotting. This gave them not only the opportunity of recording the numbers of the many great steam locomotives that thundered by, with steam and smoke billowing from their chimneys, but also the names of the great steam engines. James remembers steam trains with nostalgia:

> For most boys in particular, this started a dream of one day becoming a train driver. Then it would be you sitting in the driver's seat, leaning out of the window watching to see if the signals were set at green for your train to progress on its way. If you were lucky enough to live by a railway line it was an everyday thing for these trains to thunder by your home. It also meant you could get up close to the line and really see how these trains looked.

Our house had a long back garden that backed right onto the railway property with the lines on top of a steep bank. A single wire fence separated us from the railway and this was easily climbed. We sat behind a bush at the top of this bank as express trains on their way to London thundered by, mere feet away. The noise this made was terrific. It was also fun to watch the slower freight trains and, if any of these were held up at the signal just past my back garden, we could see right inside the footplate of the engine, making sure, of course, that the men on the engine didn't see us.

Paddy Curran remembers the steam trains, too:

The majesty of the steam engines as they roared and thundered along the line, displaying a frenzy of smoke and steam as they went was a joy to behold. No wonder every boy wanted to be a train driver. We used to watch the trains from close up and it was fun to place a half penny on the tracks and watch it get squashed so that it became the size of one old penny.

The steam trains were a source of entertainment that hard-pressed mums made full use of, as Sue Diaper remembers:

I remember having to look after my little brother John when we used to go into town with Mum. He used to love trains so she'd leave us in a small grassy area opposite the Civic Centre where the trains went underneath into a tunnel. I was supposed to be in charge, but John always played me up and I used to hate having to babysit him!

THE WATER

With the end of the steam era in sight, the run from Southampton's terminus station to Alton was soon covered by the traction of a diesel electric multiple unit, and the new technology spread fast. The 1950s still had one big advantage though, and that was the passage of steam trains specially run from London, coming through from Northam station to progress straight into Southampton Docks. These trains brought passengers for the many great liners waiting to convey them to the USA or away to the warmth of overseas cruise destinations. These special trains went up to Southampton's world famous Ocean Terminal, opened in July 1950 and billed as 'the most modern dockside terminal in the world' (*Britain on Film*). From there, passengers were funnelled on board their waiting ship.

The *Normandy* at Southampton Docks in the early 1980s. The engine was built in 1893 for the London and South Western Railway (LSWR) and worked as a dock shunter. It was withdrawn from service and sold in 1963. (Photograph courtesy Richard de Jong, with thanks to Mike Roussel)

The Ocean Terminal, the pride and joy of Southampton Docks, in the mid-1950s. (Photo courtesy of Julie Green)

Liners based at Southampton during the 1950s included the *Queen Mary*, *Queen Elizabeth*, *The United States* and *The France*. Travel on the boat trains was the start of a luxury passage across the Atlantic, on trains pulled by large steam engines with luxurious Pullman coaches, often carrying very rich and important people.

The Ocean Terminal cost £750,000 to create and stood along an almost quarter-mile (1,297ft) stretch of Quay Dock, and was 111ft wide. The Prime Minister, the Right Honourable Clement Atlee, opened the terminal. It boasted facilities that were astonishingly ahead of its time. It had two floors; the upper floor was for passenger handling and the ground floor was devoted to their baggage. First-class passengers, and those considered VIPs, had their own separate area. The upper floor offered much that would not be out of place in today's airline terminals. Shops and buffets, banking facilities, writing rooms and telecommunications services were all available, continuing the luxury and glamour that enveloped the whole cruise concept at the time. Liners would come alongside the terminal, and six hydraulically operated telescopic gangways swung out from the upper level of the terminal and up to 2,000 passengers could be disembarked, head through customs and be off on boat trains within an hour, their baggage being unloaded to the lower level and then sent by conveyor-belt upstairs. The terminal's railway platforms were capable of coping with two boat trains at the same time. The Ocean Terminal was demolished in 1983, a victim of the rise in popularity of flying and the decline of the great liners.

The liners were as famous as the people they carried. The Cunard White Star's *Queen Mary* was beloved of many. She had been plying the seas since 1936. She won the Blue Riband, awarded for the fastest crossing of the Atlantic, in both 1936 and 1938. Rock Hudson travelled on her as a young Hollywood star and Dave Wooders remembers meeting the legendary Judy Garland while serving aboard her:

> Lisa Minnelli was travelling with her mum, Judy Garland. As a commi waiter in the first class restaurant, you would be asked to do teas for the kids. I can remember Judy Garland bringing Liza down and I was feeding her jelly and blancmange and sandwiches. I was sixteen and working on the *Queen Mary*.

In 1957, it was the turn of Hopalong Cassidy to visit Britain via Southampton. He arrived with his wife on board the liner SS *United States*. They were here for a holiday and were met by thrilled young children who loved watching Hopalong in his Western films.

Not everyone who travelled on the great liners of the time was rich or famous though. They also carried families who were emigrating to the USA, or to Australia as a '£10 Pom'. Australia had a forty-year policy of increasing the white population of the country to enlarge its economic potential. The cost of a ticket on an Australia-bound liner for an adult was £10 and children went for free. Thousands of people migrated, drawn by promises of a better life than that offered in the UK. Di Baker has first-hand experience of this:

> I remember going to my Aunt's to help clear up before they took up their £10 Pom passage. I think that this was 1955.
>
> The most distressing thing was that one evening after the children had gone to bed, my uncle had a bonfire to get rid of things that he did not want taken. As I watched from the bedroom window, he took my cousin's teddy bear and threw it into the fire. It landed on the top, gave an amazingly loud grunt and toppled into the flames. The image stayed with me for years, long after we had waved goodbye to our relations at the docks.

For those who could not afford a trip on a cruise ship, they could have an entertaining day out cruising around the harbour to see the docks in action and the liners from the water. Tickets on the Favourite Boats from the Royal Pier were 2s 6d for an adult and 1s 3d for children. The harbour cruises were a favourite family treat.

The docks had been vital to the war effort and were the departure point for troops on D Day. By the 1950s, they were busy with such imports as coal, Spanish sherry, New Zealand cheeses, grapes from Cyprus, melons from Israel, more than 75,000 tons a year of timber from Russia, Finland and Canada, the annual 2.5 million animal carcasses from New Zealand, which went straight into cold storage at the docks, and the 5 million banana stems that streamed off the merchant ships at 240 stems a minute, directly on to waiting trains for onward shipment. It could take ten days to unload a consignment of timber, which was then moved on by barge to yards on the Itchen and at Redbridge. The army of dockers also loaded shipments of such items as cars, Sunbeam trolleybus chassis (destined for the Johannesburg Municipal Tramways Department) and steel cables. As Paddy Curran comments: 'So many people seemed to be involved with the docks in one capacity or other. The ships would be banked two or three abreast and the air would be punctuated by the sound of their huge horns.'

Brian Stansbridge remembers that the 'Stevedores families always had fruit from crates that had been "accidentally" dropped!' James remembers something similar:

Chris Newman's grandfather, William Sawyer, at work in Southampton Docks at Corralls' Phoenix Wharf in the late 1950s. The engine is the *Corrall Queen*, formerly the *Normandy*, which was used to transport coal through the docks. He treated it like a baby, and would polish it until it shone. (Photo courtesy of Chris Newman)

While working at Montague Meyers' timber yard in the docks there was a rail yard right behind the works. Every so often these were full of rail trucks that were loaded with ripe bananas. They were no good for onward transport to the many fruit shops in the country because they had ripened on the way over here and would have been no good to go on sale, so these ripe ones were sent for destruction or pig food. When this happened, however, the cry of "Bananas" went up and all of the younger youths, myself certainly included, made a dash for these trucks and eagerly climbed in. All of us then gorged ourselves on this free bounty, so much so that for weeks afterwards not one of us could even look at another banana.

War though was never far away and it was not long before Southampton was to ring to the sound of marching feet and barked orders once more. Known in America as the 'forgotten war', because of the lack of public attention it received, the Korean War involved America and her allies in yet another destructive phase of history.

The 38th parallel was the dividing line between North and South Korea after the Second World War. The Soviets controlled the north and the Americans the south. The two failed to hold reunifying elections and the north became communist and the south capitalist. By 1950, the first shots of the war were being heard as North Korea invaded its southern counterpart and Britain was catapulted into war once again, as part of the United Nations' force. Southampton's docks braced for what was to come.

The UK sent 14,200 troops to Korea. According to *Pathé News* at the time, 1,200 men from the 1st Gloucestershire Regiment and the 55th Independent Squadron Royal Engineers, RAC, boarded the troopship *Empire Windrush* at Southampton in 1950. Families lined the dockside to wave them off. The *Empire Windrush* had been taken from the Germans as a war prize during the Second World War and was the ship used to transport the first influx of workers from the Caribbean in 1948. Afterwards a troopship, it plied the seas between Southampton and Kure during and immediately after the end of the Korean War. It was reduced to a burnt-out shell and subsequently sank on its last trip from Kure on 30 March 1954, when it was filled with the war wounded and families. They were all rescued but four of the engine room staff perished.

Many of the service men who served in Korea were National Service personnel. According to *Pathé News*, 70 per cent of the Royal Warwickshire Regiment who embarked in Southampton in 1953 were serving their two years for Queen and country.

Southampton was also the port many returning prisoners of war came through and was therefore the scene of family reunions, such as after the arrivals of the *Asturias* on 16 September 1953 and the *Empire Orwell* on 14 October. The homecomings though did not generate the mass celebrations that had characterised those of the Second World War returnees, just a few short years before. The returning Gloucester Regiment were given an official reception on their return, but the bunting and flag waving that was characteristic of the previous conflict was missing. These former prisoners came back to private family celebrations of their safe return.

FLYING BOATS

Local children would take advantage of the wonderful view of the docks that Mayflower Park offered, and they would often sit and watch the coming and goings of the Flying Boats. The children also knew these graceful aeroplanes as 'seaplanes' because they took off and landed on water. James remembers them well:

We spent a lot of time in Mayflower Park because we could get such a great view of the mighty liners that were so often to be seen in the docks. The funnels of the *Queen Mary* or *Queen Elizabeth* could be seen from miles away and you only had to count how many there were to know whether it was the Mary or the Lizzie that was in – the *Queen Mary* having three and the *Queen Elizabeth* two. But we loved to watch the seaplanes as they took off and landed on the water, sea spraying up as they landed on it. It was a sight we never got tired of.

When my friends and I were all about twelve years old in 1953, we were members of the Belgrave Road Boys Club that met once a week in the Belgrave Road Hall. We were taken on tours of some of Southampton's famous places with the club. Among these was a tour of the docks. We got right up close to some of the most famous liners in the world, as well as cargo ships from this country and around the world. It was all very exciting! Suddenly, we were given the news that a flying boat was due to come in at any moment. Coming from a maritime city, we were used to seeing boats of all different sizes, but not one of us had ever seen one flying. The excitement mounted by the minute as we waited for this phenomenon to unfold. Then our guide said, 'Here she is boys!' Looking to where he pointed our disappointment was huge, because what he was pointing at was a seaplane. That, of course, was the name we knew for these planes but the correct title for them was Flying Boats because they took off and landed on water. It made sense of course, but each one of us would so have loved to see a real boat flying over us and landing in the docks.

The flying boats stopped flying in and out of Southampton in 1958.

AEROPLANES

In the mid and late 1950s it was possible to go to Southampton Airport at Eastleigh and see the huge car-carrying planes belonging to Silver City Airways. These huge aircraft, Bristol Freighter Mk 21s and Mk 32 Superfreighters, acted as air ferries, carrying cars across the Channel to Deauville and Cherbourg and to Guernsey in the Channel Islands. The services were all moved to Bournemouth in 1959 because of the poor condition of the runway at Southampton.

James remembers outings to watch the aeroplanes loading, in an age when the roll-on, roll-off ferry was still an idea for the future:

> It was such a wonderful sight to watch the cars being loaded aboard. The front of the aircraft opened up and a ramp was lowered to the ground. Cars were then driven up this ramp and secured inside the aircraft ready for transportation.

STEAM ROLLERS

Many of Southampton's roads were still unsurfaced in the early 1950s, or were subject to yet-to-be-repaired damage left over from the Second World War. Small children on their way to school were often frightened by the noise of men using pneumatic drills for digging up the roads. They would work for hours and children would rush past them with their hands firmly clamped over their ears. The end product of this work was that the new road surfaces were laid and then was flattened down. What joy this was! Children thrilled to the sight and sound of the huge steamrollers that went backwards and forwards smoothing and levelling as they went.

They were steam powered, of course, with a small firebox that had to be tended, just like a steam train engine. Besides the two huge back wheels, they had a massive roller in front that executed the job perfectly. Naturally, children were very wary when near these giant machines. Many times in school, when being taught about road safety, the old maxim was drummed into every boy and girl in class, bringing a shudder: 'If you don't look right, left, then right again, to make sure the road is clear, you might end up under a steam roller.'

CARS

In 1950s Southampton, cars were starting to make a more definite appearance. They were mostly black and had a wide running board on both sides. For children though it was still perfectly safe for them to play in the road as these cars were few and far between and seldom drove down roads where kids were playing. After all, when Billy the Kid was in a shoot out with Sherriff Pat Garret and his posse, the last thing he wanted was to have to hold his fire while a car passed by!

OUTINGS

For many people the concept of going on holiday was a dream that could not be afforded. Days out were the most that could be hoped for. Di Baker remembers one of these trips in particular:

Lots of peoples' works would have a summer outing when we would go on a charabanc and sing songs. The police outing used to be to Sandbanks and everyone would run out of the water and take shelter when it started to rain!

Paddy Curran also has memories of his family days out:

> We would get to go on a train once a year – our annual holiday consisted of a day out to Bournemouth on the train. I remember floating my plastic boat up the little stream that runs through the park there.

Gill Holloway remembers an early teenage holiday at Chesil Beach Holiday Camp in Weymouth:

> It was the first big holiday for Margaret and me, when she was eighteen and I was seventeen. We were life-long friends, both only children, and met when we were three. I remember that there were some people from Birmingham at the camp and they kicked up if there was salad. It was not 'proper food' according to them. There were organised walks, a camp song, evening dances where the 'Paul Jones' was popular for getting to know people. The Paul Jones was a particular piece of music with ladies in a circle travelling clockwise and men forming an outer circle travelling anti-clockwise, then when the music stopped you partnered the person you were facing and enjoyed the next dance together and the process was repeated. A crowd of we teenagers went for a very late walk and returned to find the camp locked so we managed to climb back through a bedroom window.

Janet Bowen was one of the few whose family could afford a holiday:

> Sometimes we went on holiday in a taxi! This could have been for several reasons – there were three young children and Dad was not in good health. We went to Weymouth mostly and stayed with an Aunt. Days on the beach are very much remembered and Dad's photos help those memories.

Gill Holloway and friends at the Chesil Beach Holiday Camp in Weymouth in 1957. As you can see, teenagers were being teenagers! (Image courtesy of Gill Holloway)

Eileen de Lisle Long remembers the thrill of her first overseas holiday:

> Mum had taken a part-time job as a school dinner supervisor. Dad and Mum between them had saved enough money to take us abroad for a holiday. We visited eight countries in Europe and I couldn't believe it, I was so excited. I felt like a film star staying in posh hotels. This excitement lasted for years and that very first trip abroad with the family will always be my favourite holiday. Previously, all our holidays were taken in Devon and Cornwall staying in guesthouses and caravans – working-class families in the fifties couldn't afford holidays abroad.

Janet Bowen and her parents on Woolston railway station, taken in 1952.
(Image courtesy of Janet Bowen)

As the decade progressed, so too did innovation, such as the
hovercraft which arrived in Southampton when Sir Christopher
Cockerell tested his 'air cushion vehicle' off Cowes in 1959. This
invention wowed adults and children alike and was a symbol
of what the future could hold. For children growing up in
Southampton in the 1950s, the coming decade offered a wealth
of possibilities. For kids who took change in their stride, there was
much to look forward to!

EPILOGUE

Growing up in 1950s Southampton was a maelstrom of different experiences for the children of the town. Many could remember the war and the terrors it had brought. Some children would never get over the effects of the conflict. The notorious case of Derek Bentley in Croydon, hanged at the age of nineteen for the murder of a policeman, could be said to be an extreme case in point. At the age of seven, he had been in the family air-raid shelter when it took a direct hit. He had to be dug out of the rubble – just weeks later he lost his sister, grandmother and aunt to another bomb. At the age of eleven he was asleep at home when a doodlebug caught the flat. An epileptic, his education was disrupted and he left school all but illiterate. Although his sad case did not happen in Southampton, it offers an insight into how wartime conditions may have affected kids in the town. How many went off the rails because of their wartime experiences is not part of the scope of this book, but is worthy of mention.

All could see the ravages the war had left – both in terms of the physical damage wartime bombing had inflicted and in the invisible costs, in terms of shattered nerves, post-traumatic stress and the toll it took on the adult population. The entire decade was dominated by the need to get over the war and move on.

Nevertheless, through talking to the people of Southampton who were children in the 1950s, it is obvious that there is a great deal of affection for the period. Life was slower, quieter and there seemed to be a clearer sense of what was right and what was wrong. Social norms ruled and those who stepped outside of these were ostracized. This was most obvious in the matter of law and order. If a person went to prison, their whole family suffered. The murder of Elsie Phippard on 22 May 1954 by her husband Ernest – who was insanely jealous of the incestuous relationship he was convinced was going on between Elsie and their eldest son George, eighteen – was a shocking case that stands out in Southampton in the period. Ernest worked at the Pirelli cable works in the town and he, his wife and their family of five children, aged between six and eighteen, lived in Chestnut Road, Shirley Warren. Ernest and Elsie had argued many times about the fixation he held and no amount of counselling helped. On the day in question, George came home to discover his father standing over his dead mother with blood on his face. Ernest was later found to be certifiably insane and delusional, and was found guilty of Elsie's murder but insane and was detained in custody. The five children had been subjected to a family life in which incest, insanity and discord were all a part and this had led, in time, to the loss of one parent at the hands of the other. For this family, the 1950s certainly was not the happy decade it has been portrayed by many in this book.

Going to school is never popular with children no matter what the decade, but those born in the 1950s who spoke to the authors revealed nostalgia for their schooldays that is touching, despite the stern discipline that was a fact of life. Many could remember their teachers' names and much detail of their school days.

During the 1950s, children could play as perhaps children have not been able to do in later decades – there was a sense of innocence that has largely been lost in the time since.

This book has looked at all manner of areas of growing up in the 1950s in Southampton. As researchers of the era, the authors hope that *A 1950s Southampton Childhood* has at least touched on the decade, to give as complete a picture of the time as possible and in doing so, have succeeded in bringing the 1950s to a twenty-first-century audience in some small manner.

BIBLIOGRAPHY

BOOKS

Anon, *Memories of Southampton*, (Halifax, True North Books Limited, 1999)

Anon, *More Memories of Southampton*, (Halifax, True North Books Limited, 2002)

Arnott, A., *Maritime Southampton* (Derby, Breedon Books Publishing Company Limited, 2002)

Brown, J., *Southampton Murder Victims* (Derby, DB Publishing, 2010)

Bull, D. and B. Brunskell, *Match of the Millennium*, (Hagiology, 2000)

Haisman, D., *Raised on the Titanic* (Boolarong Press, 2002)

Legg, P., *Southampton Then & Now* (Stroud, The History Press, 2010)

Legg, P., *Under the Queen's Colours* (Stroud, The History Press, 2012)

Moody, B., *150 Years of Southampton Docks* (Southampton, Kingfisher Railway Productions, 1988)

Morris, C., *Hants and Dorset: A History* (Croydon, DTS Publishing Ltd, 1973)

Shephard, J.C., *Southampton's Cinemas* (Wakefield, Mercia Cinema Society, 1994)

Trow, M.J., *War Crimes, Underworld Britain in the Second World War* (Yorkshire, Pen and Sword Military, 2008)

White, B., S. Jemima and D. Hyslop, *Dream Palaces Going to the Pictures in Southampton* (Southampton City Council, 1996)

WEBSITES

www.albertschatzphd.com
www.archive.org
www.archiveshub.ac.uk
www.andmas.co.uk
www.bbc.co.uk
www.bookdrum.com
www.british-history.ac.uk
www.britishpathe.com
www.bulleidsociety.org
www.davidstjohn.co.uk
www.dmcginley.com
www.edwardianteddyboy.com
www.focusbiz.co.uk
www.friendsreunited.com
www.guardian.co.uk
www.jakesimpkin.org
www.localhistories.org
www.mayflower.org.uk
www.museumvictoria.com.au
www.ofcom.org.uk

www.pelhampuppets.uk.com
www.petergould.co.uk
www.plimsoll.org
www.prints.paphotos.com
www.providentfinancial.com
www.qlocal.co.uk
www.queenmary.com
www.rediffusion.info
www.royal.gov.uk
www.shirleyjuniorschool.org.uk
www.silvercityairways.com
www.socyberty.com
www.southampton.ac.uk
www.southampton.gov.uk
www.southamptonuk.co.uk
www.telegraph.co.uk
www.turnipnet.com
www.tvhistory.tv
www.uktv.co.uk
www.wondersofyouth.co.uk